# WOMEN IN SPORT

## 50 FEARLESS ATHLETES WHO PLAYED TO WIN

### WRITTEN AND ILLUSTRATED BY RACHEL IGNOTOFSKY

wren & rook

# CONTENTS

# WOMEN IN SPORT

'The weaker sex!' It wasn't the first time those untrue words were said, and it wouldn't be the last. It's what Bobby Riggs, a former tennis champ, said about women in 1973. But tennis player Billie Jean King stood up to this bully. With masterful skill, physical strength and a strong sense of self-worth, Billie Jean would change the world with her tennis racket.

Throughout history, women have been stereotyped as weak, and routinely excluded from sporting competitions, gyms, teams and clubs. With no arena in which to prove themselves fit and strong, it was hard for women to fight this sexism. Of course, this stereotype did not just apply to sport. Women have been denied educational, civic, business and leadership opportunities and have had to prove they are just as smart and hardworking as men. Female athletes have had to fight the most basic stereotype of all: that women's bodies are inherently not as strong or capable as men's. Their progress has been truly inspiring.

During the 1970s, the feminist movement was in full swing in the United States, United Kingdom and other developed nations. Women were demanding equal pay and equal opportunities. In 1972, the United States passed a law making it illegal for US schools to discriminate in funding based on gender. For the first time, many colleges and universities began funding women's sports programmes and giving out women's sports scholarships. Finally, women could pursue their athletic passions and show the world their true strength.

The backlash was inevitable. Many people still thought women should do only traditional 'ladylike' activities. Bobby Riggs wanted to prove that women had no place in sport by beating the best female tennis player, Billie Jean King. In 1973, he challenged her to a 'battle of the sexes' tennis match. At first she declined. But when Bobby beat Grand Slam winner Margaret Court in the 'Mother's Day massacre' match, Billie Jean understood there was more at stake than just a game.

The whole world was watching as Billie Jean and Bobby entered the tennis court. Winning would not be enough; she would have to wipe the floor with him. And she did: the score was 6-4, 6-3, 6-3. Billie threw her racket into the air in victory as the crowd went wild!

SHE HAS SET A WORLD RECORD!

SHE IS STRONG!

SHE IS THE FASTEST!

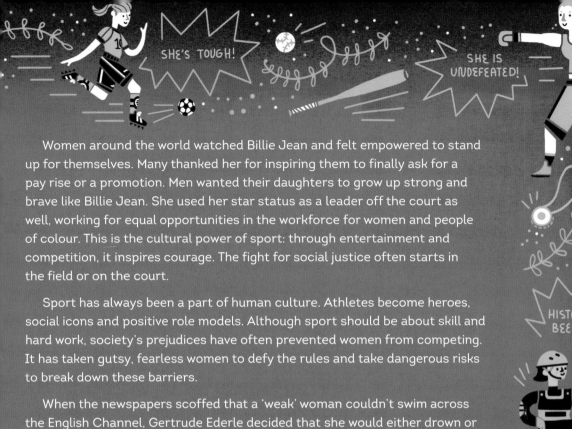

Women around the world watched Billie Jean and felt empowered to stand up for themselves. Many thanked her for inspiring them to finally ask for a pay rise or a promotion. Men wanted their daughters to grow up strong and brave like Billie Jean. She used her star status as a leader off the court as well, working for equal opportunities in the workforce for women and people of colour. This is the cultural power of sport: through entertainment and competition, it inspires courage. The fight for social justice often starts in the field or on the court.

Sport has always been a part of human culture. Athletes become heroes, social icons and positive role models. Although sport should be about skill and hard work, society's prejudices have often prevented women from competing. It has taken gutsy, fearless women to defy the rules and take dangerous risks to break down these barriers.

When the newspapers scoffed that a 'weak' woman couldn't swim across the English Channel, Gertrude Ederle decided that she would either drown or triumph. She triumphed — and set a new world record in 1926. When Althea Gibson, a black woman, played tennis during the segregation era, her talent was so undeniable that she was able to cross the colour line and become the first African American to win Wimbledon. Her success helped the civil rights movement and paved the way for athletic greats like Serena Williams. When Sue Sally Hale was told women were not allowed to play polo, she disguised herself as a man for 20 years to play the sport she loved.

These are just a few examples of female athletes who proved their worth as individuals, showing the world what women can do and creating opportunities for future generations. There are still problems in women's sport, such as a lack of funding and media coverage, and unequal pay. But with each generation, women accomplish feats that challenge the status quo. This book is filled with stories of little girls who grew up to achieve their dreams — stories of women who pushed themselves to the limit, did the impossible and became legends.

# TIMELINE

Throughout history, women have fought for the right to compete by proving themselves with strength, endurance and impressive wins. From being forbidden to watch sporting events to becoming fierce athletes, let's celebrate how far women in sport have come!

## AROUND 776 BCE

First ancient Olympic Games. Women are not allowed to compete, and married women are forbidden to watch the games on penalty of death.

## 1866

Vassar College, a top US women's university, creates an all-female baseball team.

## 1926

Gertrude Ederle becomes the first woman to swim the English Channel.

## 1950

Althea Gibson is the first black tennis player to compete at an all-white country club in US Nationals.

## 1972

In the US, funding for school sport was weighted to boys' teams. In 1972, Title IX of the Education Amendments Act outlaws gender discrimination in school activities.

## 1978

UNESCO declares that sport is a 'fundamental right for all'. Although it's an often-overlooked right, people worldwide are working hard to ensure girls and women everywhere have access to physical activity.

**1896**

Women are banned from competing in the first modern Olympic Games, but 'Melpomene' is rumoured to run the marathon unofficially.

**1900**

First modern Olympic Games that allows women to compete.

**1964**

Before the Civil Rights Act, African Americans did not have equal protection under the law. In 1964, racial segregation in the USA becomes unconstitutional. Although the effects of segregation are still felt, people of colour have more opportunities in sport.

**1966**

Bobbi Gibb is the first woman to run the Boston Marathon by sneaking in and disguising herself.

**1991**

FIFA creates the first women's football World Cup.

**1996**

The Women's National Basketball Association (WNBA) is established.

**NOW**

Female athletes are still fighting for equal access, exposure and pay, but they are breaking records and winning big!

FIRST WOMAN TO COMPETE AT THE WORLD FIGURE-SKATING CHAMPIONSHIPS.

WON GOLD IN THE 1908 OLYMPICS.

INSPIRED THE CREATION OF THE FEMALE CATEGORY IN FIGURE-SKATING.

'MRS SYERS ... IS STILL IN A CLASS BY HERSELF. THE WONDERFUL ACCURACY OF HER FIGURES, COMBINED WITH PERFECT CARRIAGE AND MOVEMENT, WAS THE CHIEF FEATURE OF THE MORNING'S SKATING.'
—THE OFFICIAL REPORT OF THE PRINCE'S SKATING CLUB AT THE 1902 WORLD CHAMPIONSHIPS

# MADGE SYERS

## FIGURE-SKATER

COMPETED IN HER FIRST WORLD CHAMPIONSHIP IN A FULL-LENGTH SKIRT.

EXIST CRITICS OF THE LADIES' WORLD CHAMPIONSHIP WERE AFRAID THE JUDGES WOULD FALL IN LOVE WITH THE SKATERS.

WON BRITAIN'S 1903 AND 1904 NATIONAL CHAMPIONSHIPS.

Florence Madeline 'Madge' Cave was born in 1881 and grew up in Britain. During the winter, both men and women enjoyed figure-skating, but women were not allowed to participate in any of the competitions. Many were afraid that competitive physical activities would be too much stress for a woman's 'weak' body. But Madge was such an amazing figure-skater, she gained notoriety and respect within the skating community.

In 1899, Madge married fellow skater Edgar Syers; he coached her to leave behind the rigid English style of figure-skating and started teaching her the more fluid International style. She was a natural. Madge was ready to compete in the 1902 World Championships, which only men could take part in at that time. Defiant, she entered the competition anyway. Officials wanted to throw her out, but they soon realised that there was no explicit rule excluding women. Still, they protested about her entry. But with no actual rule to exclude her, and considering her great reputation on the ice, officials had to let her compete.

Madge needed to prove that she belonged in the rink just as much as the male skaters. Triumphantly, she came in second place, securing her place as a competitive skater. Recognising her amazing performance, the International Skating Union created a ladies' World Championship. Madge competed in the first ever ISU Championships for Ladies' Figure-Skating in 1906. She won, and won again the following year. Next, she headed for the Olympics!

The International Olympic Committee (IOC) had first allowed women to compete in 1900, but many events were still men-only. The 1908 Olympic Games included figure-skating for the first time, and it was open to women. Madge won gold for her solo performance and bronze with Edgar in the pairs event.

Tragically, Madge's life was cut short; she developed an acute heart inflammation and died in 1917 at age 35. Her bravery and excellence helped future women show their talents to the world.

BEGAN THE TREND OF SKATING IN CALF-LENGTH SKIRTS SO JUDGES COULD SEE HER FOOTWORK.

CO-WROTE *THE ART OF SKATING: INTERNATIONAL STYLE* WITH EDGAR.

FIRST WOMAN TO WIN TWO MEDALS IN FIGURE-SKATING AT THE SAME OLYMPIC GAMES.

SKYDIVED OVER 1,000 TIMES.

FIRST PERSON TO DO A FREE-FALL SKYDIVE.

FIRST WOMAN TO PARACHUTE FROM AN AEROPLANE.

'WHEN I SAW THAT BALLOON GO UP, AND I GAWKED AT IT AS IT ASCENDED INTO THE HEAVENS, I KNEW I'D NEVER BE THE SAME.' —TINY BROADWICK

# TINY BROADWICK

## SKYDIVER

Georgia Ann Thompson had been nicknamed 'Tiny' for as long as she could remember. She was under five feet tall and weighed less than 41 kg, but that didn't stop her from taking big risks. In the course of her skydiving career she would break bones, get tangled in trees and even land on top of a moving train. She always went back to the sky — as she said, 'There is no real fun except far up in the air.'

Tiny was born in 1893 in North Carolina, USA. By age 15, she was already a widow, left to support her baby daughter by working at a local cotton mill. Her life would change forever when the carnival came to town. She was transfixed by the hot air balloon act, where performers jumped from the balloon with parachutes. Tiny begged the group leader, Charles Broadwick, to let her join the act, and in 1908 she made her first parachute jump. She had found her calling. Charles adopted Tiny, and together they toured the country so she could jump from balloons for excited crowds.

Although parachutes made aeroplane flight safer, the military and the public did not understand or trust this new invention. To help change attitudes about parachute safety, in 1913, Tiny was the first woman to parachute from an aeroplane. With the help of pilot and aviation specialist Glenn Martin, she jumped from a plane at over 600 metres up in the air. Impressed by her reputation, the US military engaged Tiny to advise the aeronautics corps during the First World War. Her jumps helped create the US Air Force's standard practices for how to use parachutes. In 1914, Tiny completed the first free-fall jump in history: a military test jump went awry and her parachute's lines got tangled on the plane's tail. She had to cut herself free, but managed to land safely!

Throughout her parachuting career, Tiny continued to do death-defying stunts. After over 1,000 jumps, Tiny developed ankle problems, and she retired in 1922 at age 29. She died in 1978, a legendary figure in aviation and a pioneer of one of the most exciting extreme sports.

OPENED AND RELEASED MULTIPLE PARACHUTES DURING HER CIRCUS ACT.

FIRST WOMAN TO PARACHUTE INTO A BODY OF WATER, LANDING IN LAKE MICHIGAN.

AWARDED THE US GOVERNMENT PIONEER AVIATION AWARD AND THE JOHN GLENN MEDAL.

CALLED 'THE FIRST LADY OF PARACHUTING.'

MEMBER OF THE 'EARLY BIRDS OF AVIATION' WHO FLEW SOLO BEFORE DECEMBER 17, 1916.

ONE OF HER PARACHUTES IS IN THE NATIONAL AIR AND SPACE MUSEUM.

IN THE CANADIAN SPORTS HALL OF FAME.

300

NAMED CANADA'S ATHLETE OF THE HALF-CENTURY (1900–1950).

CALLED THE SUPER WOMAN OF LADIES' ICE HOCKEY.

'THE MODERN GIRL IS A BETTER WORKER AND A HAPPIER WOMAN BY REASON OF THE HEALTHY PLEASURE SHE TAKES IN TENNIS, LACROSSE, SWIMMING, RUNNING, JUMPING AND OTHER SPORTS.' — BOBBIE ROSENFELD

# BOBBIE ROSENFELD

## ATHLETICS, ICE HOCKEY, TENNIS AND SOFTBALL PLAYER

HE SET NATIONAL RECORDS FOR RUNNING LONG JUMP, DISCUS AND STANDING BROAD JUMP DURING THE OLYMPIC TRIALS.

#1 DAD

T WAS HARD O FIND SPORTS LOTHES FOR WOMEN, SO SHE USED ROPE O HOLD UP HER SHORTS AND WORE HER DAD'S SHIRTS.

YOU CAN DO IT, JEAN!

ENTERED THE OOM RACE IN THE 1928 OLYMPICS JUST TO SUPPORT HER TEAMMATE, JEAN THOMPSON.

Fanny 'Bobbie' Rosenfeld was born in 1904 in Russia, and her family moved to Canada when she was a baby. As a teenager, Bobbie played softball and was known for her speed. During a softball tournament, her teammates encouraged Bobbie to enter a nearby 100-yard race. Still dressed for softball, she ran to victory, winning her first sports medal and dethroning the Canadian national champion. This started her athletic career, and by the mid-1920s, she was a top Canadian women's sprinter.

1928 was the first year women were allowed to compete in athletics events at the Olympics, though only on a trial basis. At the time, many doctors believed the female body could not handle the physicality of Olympic competition, and tried to cancel the events. The women at these Games weren't just competing for medals — they wanted to prove they belonged at the Olympics, and every strong performance helped. Bobbie won a gold medal in the 4x100 m relay and set a new world record with her team. She also won silver in the 100 m race. But the achievements of Bobbie and others did not convince everyone that women deserved to compete in all the athletics events. After a woman allegedly collapsed at the end of the 800 m race (in which Bobbie was fifth), and although the first three finishers set world record-breaking times, the Olympic committee banned women from competing in the 800 m race for the next 32 years.

Bobbie continued her multifaceted sports career, but in 1929, she began to suffer from bouts of painful arthritis. Within two years she was back to playing softball and ice hockey. In 1931, she was the best hitter on her softball team and the 'most outstanding player' on her hockey team. Around 1933, her arthritis flared up again and she had to retire from sports completely.

Bobbie became an amazing sports writer with the Toronto newspaper *Globe & Mail*, where she was a fierce advocate for women's athletics. She died in 1969, a legend on and off the field.

WON THE 1924 TORONTO LADIES' GRASS COURT TENNIS CHAMPIONSHIP.

NICKNAMED 'BOBBIE' FOR HER BOBBED HAIRCUT.

PLAYED IN CANADA'S NATIONAL BASKETBALL FINALS TWICE WITH TORONTO'S YOUNG WOMEN'S HEBREW ASSOCIATION.

THE BOBBIE ROSENFELD AWARD IS GIVEN TO THE BEST CANADIAN FEMALE ATHLETE OF THE YEAR.

HONOURED IN THE INTERNATIONAL SWIMMING HALL OF FAME.

GOLD MEDALLIST IN THE 1924 OLYMPICS.

FIRST WOMAN TO SWIM THE ENGLISH CHANNEL.

'WHEN SOMEBODY TELLS ME I CANNOT DO SOMETHING, THAT IS WHEN I DO IT.' — GERTRUDE EDERLE

# GERTRUDE EDERLE

## DISTANCE SWIMMER

Gertrude Caroline Ederle swam her way into America's heart. Born in 1905 in New York City, Gertrude started swimming very young and became one of the most accomplished swimmers of all time. At the 1924 Olympics, Gertrude won a gold and two bronze medals. Gertrude liked racing, but her real interest was long-distance swimming. She swam from the docks of Lower Manhattan's Battery to Sandy Hook, New Jersey: 28 km in 7 hours and 11 minutes, a new world record!

Gertrude wanted to do the impossible: become the first woman to swim across the English Channel. Newspapers scoffed at the idea. The *London Daily News* wrote, 'Women must admit that in a contest of physical skill, speed and endurance, they must remain forever the weaker sex'. Only five men in history had successfully swum the 36.2-km-wide Channel. Gertrude wanted to beat the fastest time, swum by Enrique Tirabocchi: 16 hours, 33 minutes.

Her first attempt, in 1925, was a disaster. After nearly nine hours of swimming, she became seasick and was pulled into a boat. But she still wanted to prove that she could do it. One year of intense training later, Gertrude was back.

That day, the water was so dangerous that even boats had trouble. She was set off course many times by the choppy waters and couldn't use the currents to her advantage. Gertrude decided that she would either swim or drown, but she would never quit. She persevered and made it across the Channel in 14 hours, 31 minutes — beating the world record by two hours!

Gertrude was an instant sensation and returned home to one of the largest parades New York City had ever seen. She proved that a woman could succeed under the most extreme conditions, and because of her success, swimming became one of the most popular sports for women throughout the 1920s and 30s. Her record remained unbroken for 24 years.

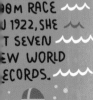

DURING ONE 300M RACE IN 1922, SHE SET SEVEN NEW WORLD RECORDS.

SHE COVERED HERSELF IN OLIVE OIL, LANOLIN AND LARD TO KEEP WARM WHILE SWIMMING THE CHANNEL.

SHE BECAME PARTIALLY DEAF FROM ALL OF HER TIME IN THE ENGLISH CHANNEL.

NICKNAMED 'QUEEN OF THE WAVES' AND 'AMERICA'S BEST GIRL'.

WAS FEATURED IN MOVIES AND VAUDEVILLE ACTS.

SET MORE THAN 29 WORLD AND NATIONAL RECORDS.

IN RETIREMENT, SHE TAUGHT DEAF CHILDREN HOW TO SWIM.

IN THE INTERNATIONAL SWIMMING HALL OF FAME.

FEATURED IN SEVERAL OF THE FIRST SWIMMING MOVIES EVER MADE.

BECAME THE YOUNGEST OLYMPIC GOLD MEDALLIST OF HER TIME AT AGE 14.

'MY MOST UNFORGETTABLE EXPERIENCE WOULD HAVE TO BE AS THE YOUNGEST MEMBER OF THE FIRST AMERICAN WOMEN'S OLYMPIC SWIMMING AND DIVING TEAM IN 1920.' — AILEEN RIGGIN

# AILEEN RIGGIN

## DIVER AND SWIMMER

HER FATHER WAS IN THE NAVY AND SHE LEARNED TO SWIM IN THE PHILIPPINES AT AGE 6.

WAS FEATURED IN THE FIRST UNDERWATER MOVIE IN 1922 AND THE FIRST SLOW-MOTION SWIMMING MOVIE IN 1923.

INDUCTED INTO THE INTERNATIONAL SWIMMING HALL OF FAME IN 1967.

Aileen Riggin, later known by her married name Aileen Soule, was born in 1906 in Rhode Island, USA. Around age 11, her doctor recommended swimming to rebuild her strength after a bout of flu. Diving became her new favourite activity. Many people at the time feared diving was too dangerous for women and girls, and most pools would not let Aileen practise, so she had to be creative. She trained for the US Olympic trials at an outdoor tidal pool, where divers had to time their dives with the height of the tide. When conditions were perfect, the diving board was 3 m above the water, just like in a real Olympic pool!

Although a young girl diving was seen as scandalous, at age 14 Aileen qualified for the 1920 US Olympic diving and swimming teams. Aileen was almost excluded from the diving because of her age, but because she also qualified for the swimming team, she was allowed to travel overseas. On the 13-day voyage to Antwerp, Belgium, Aileen practised swimming in a small canvas tank filled with seawater, where she was held in place with a belt around her waist, but she couldn't practise diving at all. Conditions at the Games weren't much better because Belgium was still recovering from the First World War. The outdoor pools were so muddy, Aileen was afraid that when she dived in, she would get stuck at the bottom forever. She overcame her fears and won the gold medal for diving!

At the 1924 Olympics in Paris, Aileen again competed in both swimming and diving. She won silver for the 3 m springboard event and bronze in the 100 m backstroke, making her the first person to win medals in diving and swimming in the same Games.

Aileen made movies, performed all over the world and later became a sports writer — and she never stopped swimming. At age 85, she broke six world records for her age group at the World Masters Swimming Championships. On her death at age 96, she was the oldest living female Olympic medallist.

HER 1926 STAGE ACT INCLUDED DIVING INTO A 1.8M-DEEP GLASS TANK.

STARRED IN THE FIRST BILLY ROSE AQUACADE, A FAMOUS DANCE AND SWIM SHOW.

AT THE 1920 OLYMPICS, SHE BECAME THE YOUNGEST AMERICAN TO WIN A GOLD MEDAL.

WON A TOTAL OF 82 AMATEUR AND PROFESSIONAL GOLF TOURNAMENTS.

FOUNDING MEMBER OF THE LADIES PROFESSIONAL GOLF ASSOCIATION.

WON TWO GOLD MEDALS AND ONE SILVER IN THE 1932 OLYMPICS FOR ATHLETICS.

'MY GOAL WAS TO BE THE GREATEST ATHLETE THAT EVER LIVED. I SUPPOSE I WAS BORN WITH THE URGE TO PLAY SPORTS.' — BABE DIDRIKSON ZAHARIAS

# BABE DIDRIKSON ZAHARIAS

## GOLFER, TRACK AND FIELD ATHLETE AND BASKETBALL PLAYER

Babe Didrikson Zaharias (born Mildred Ella Didrikson) competed as a one-woman athletics team; she was also a basketball star and a golf legend. She trash-talked and proudly boasted when she won. She wrote that she was going to be 'the greatest athlete in the world. Not the greatest female athlete. The greatest athlete!'

Born in 1911, Babe grew up in Texas, USA, one of seven children. At school, Babe was the star in every sport: baseball, volleyball, swimming, tennis and basketball — you name it! Then the Employers Casualty Insurance Company of Dallas gave her a secretarial job so she would play on their amateur women's basketball team, the Golden Cyclones. The team was one of the best in the league, and she became a star.

For publicity, the company entered Babe as a one-woman team during the qualifier for the Olympics. Most teams had many athletes, each doing different events. Babe swept the competition all by herself, winning five events and tying for first in high jump. At the time, women were only allowed to compete in up to three Olympic events. Babe won gold medals and set new world records in both the javelin and the 80 m hurdles, and tied for first in the high jump, but because of her head-first technique, she was awarded silver instead of sharing the gold.

The media adored Babe, and she made so much money that she was able to support her entire family throughout the Great Depression. She then decided to try golf. Determined to become a champion, she practised until her fingers bled, hitting as many as 1,000 balls a day. She crushed the competition at the women's amateur golf circuit with a winning streak at 14 amateur tournaments from 1946–47. The Associated Press named her Female Athlete of the Year six times. She became the first woman to qualify and make the 36-hole cut in the men's 1945 PGA event. She broke gender barriers and co-founded the Ladies Professional Golf Association. She is revered as one of the greatest sportswomen ever.

HER DAD BUILT A GYM IN THEIR GARDEN SO BABE AND HER SIBLINGS COULD WORK OUT.

HATED WHEN NEWSPAPERS CALLED HER 'THE MUSCLE WOMAN'.

MET HER PRO-WRESTLER HUSBAND, GEORGE ZAHARIAS, IN 1938 WHEN THEY PLAYED TO PROMOTE THE PGA LOS ANGELES OPEN.

STRUCK OUT YANKEE PLAYER JOE DIMAGGIO DURING AN EXHIBITION GAME.

I'M RACING TO GET TO MY RACE!

IN THE OLYMPIC QUALIFIER, SHE HAD ONLY MINUTES BETWEEN EVENTS.

THE BABE DIDRIKSON ZAHARIAS MUSEUM IS IN HER HOMETOWN OF BEAUMONT, TEXAS, USA.

FIRST WOMAN TO BE RANKED A 10TH DAN IN JUDO.

FOUNDED THE SOKO JOSHI JUDO CLUB, THE FIRST JUDO CLUB FOR WOMEN.

PIONEER OF WOMEN'S JUDO; TAUGHT JUDO ALL OVER THE WORLD.

'MORE IMPORTANT [THAN TECHNIQUE] IS BEING A GOOD HUMAN BEING...
DON'T FORGET, THAT'S GOOD JUDO.' — KEIKO FUKUDA

# KEIKO FUKUDA

## JUDOKA

Keiko Fukuda was born in 1913 in Japan, granddaughter of the samurai and jujitsu master Hachinosuke Fukuda. One of his jujitsu students, Jigorō Kanō, had developed a new form of martial arts called judo. He invited Keiko to participate in his class for women at the Kodokan Judo Institute. This class was very progressive; in the 1930s, it was scandalous for a woman to make aggressive movements or to be seen spreading her legs — both necessary for martial arts. There Keiko learned not only how to pin or joint lock an opponent, but also the philosophy of being centered in mind, body and spirit.

Keiko took her first class at age 21 and was hooked. When an arranged marriage was planned for her, she had to choose between a husband and martial arts. She chose to dedicate her life to becoming an expert in judo and the gentler Ju-no-kata. In 1953, she became one of the few women to be promoted to fifth dan (a fifth-level black belt). In 1966, she moved from Japan to the San Francisco Bay Area in California, USA, where she eventually started her own dojo (martial arts studio or school). Her teaching empowered women and gave even the smallest girls the strength to flip their opponents.

For decades, the Kodokan Judo Institute would not allow women to progress beyond a fifth-level black belt. Keiko was a fifth dan for 20 years, despite her skill level. With help from her friend Shelley Fernandez, a judo student and president of the National Organization for Women's San Francisco chapter, Keiko petitioned the Kodokan to drop their sexist practices. In the early 1970s, Keiko became the first woman to reach sixth dan.

Master Keiko Fukuda taught many students and was one of the teachers responsible for popularising judo. She was awarded the placement of ninth dan in 2006. And at age 98, in 2011, she became the highest-ranking female judoka in history when USA Judo honoured her with the highest level in judo: tenth dan.

IN 1974, ESTABLSHED THE FIRST JUDO TRAINING CAMP JUST FOR WOMEN.

WROTE THE BOOKS BORN FOR THE MAT (1973) AND JU-NO-KATA (2004).

HAS A DEGREE IN JAPANESE LITERATURE FROM THE SHOWA WOMEN'S UNIVERSITY.

GAVE A KATA DEMONSTRATION FOR THE OPENING CEREMONY OF THE 1964 TOKYO OLYMPIC GAMES.

JIGORŌ KANŌ URGED HIS STUDENTS TO SPREAD HIS JUDO TEACHINGS.

BE STRONG, BE GENTLE, BE BEAUTIFUL.

GIVEN THE 'ORDER OF THE SACRED TREASURE' BY THE JAPANESE GOVERNMENT.

BOWL

CONSIDERED ONE OF THE BEST BOWLERS OF ALL TIME.

WON EIGHT US WOMEN'S OPEN TITLES, A RECORD STILL STANDING TODAY.

WON THE WORLD INVITATIONAL FIVE TIMES.

'AFTER BOWLING ONE GAME, THAT WAS IT—I WAS HOOKED ON THE SPORT.

# MARION LADEWIG

## BOWLER

I LOVE MY TOWN!

In the 1950s and 60s, bowling was all the rage. Bowling alleys were packed with amateur and professional players, and TV crews covered professional bowling tournaments. Marion Ladewig, the greatest female bowler of all time, became a US household name as 'The Queen of Bowling'.

Born Marion Margaret Van Oosten in Michigan in 1914, she started out as a softball player. At 22, she played shortstop on a local team, and her ball-throwing caught the attention of bowling centre-owner William T. Morrissey, Senior. He offered her one free game, and Marion realised this was the sport for her. In 1937, William became her coach, and she began practising daily.

LIVED IN GRAND MISSOURI RAPIDS HER WHOLE LIFE.

With dedication, her bowling average increased to 182. (Bowling a perfect game — knocking down all ten pins every round — scores a 300.) Soon she was ready for the 1941 Western Michigan Gold Pin Classic, where she won the singles title. She continued to win tournaments, and the trophies started to pile up.

WHAT'S MY LINE?

APPEARED ON AN EPISODE OF WHAT'S MY LINE IN 1964.

In 1949, Marion began a winning streak that would turn her into a bowling legend. She won first place in the National All-Star game five years in a row, from 1950 to 1954. In 1951, on her way to winning her third All-Star title, she bowled an average of 247.6 — higher than that of any other tournament player, male or female. She won the National All-Star title eight times. All the while, the cameras were rolling, and Marion became a television star!

Marion also competed in international tournaments. In 1950, she won the all-events title at the Women's International Bowling Congress. This category totals all points earned in an entire tournament, including any singles, doubles or team events. In 1955, she won the all-events title again and also the doubles title.

NAMED FEMALE BOWLER OF THE YEAR NINE TIMES.

Marion helped start the Professional Women's Bowling Association, the first all-women's organisation of its kind. She retired in 1965 but ran a bowling alley in her home town. Marion Ladewig is remembered as one of the greatest bowlers ever.

WORKED FOR BRUNSWICK BOWLING FOR 30 YEARS, TEACHING BOWLING AROUND THE WORLD.

DEMONSTRATED BOWLING AT THE 1988 SEOUL OLYMPICS.

HALL OF FAME

INDUCTED INTO THE MICHIGAN SPORTS HALL OF FAME IN 1959.

BOWL·BOWL·    ·BOWL·BOWL·

FIRST WOMAN TO PLAY BASEBALL IN A PRO MEN'S LEAGUE.

IN THE INTERNATIONAL WOMEN'S SPORTS HALL OF FAME.

PLAYED FOR THE INDIANAPOLIS CLOWNS AND THE KANSAS CITY MONARCHS.

'A WOMAN HAS HER DREAMS, TOO. WHEN YOU FINISH HIGH SCHOOL, THEY TELL A BOY TO GO OUT AND SEE THE WORLD. WHAT DO THEY TELL A GIRL? THEY TELL HER TO GO NEXT DOOR AND MARRY THE BOY THAT THEIR FAMILIES PICKED FOR HER. IT WASN'T RIGHT.' —TONI STONE

# TONI STONE

## BASEBALL PLAYER

**I AM HERE TO PLAY!**

**...WAS ASKED TO PLAY IN A SKIRT, BUT SHE REFUSED!**

Marcenia 'Toni' Lyle Stone was born in Minnesota, USA, in 1921 and grew up loving sport. She played baseball from age 10 and was often the only girl on the field. Professional women's baseball began in 1943 with the All-American Girls Baseball League, but women of colour were not allowed to join. Segregation was in effect in the United States, and it extended to sports teams. Professional men's baseball had the all-white Major League and the all-black Negro American League. It was 1947 when Jackie Robinson became the first black man to play on a Major League team. Toni was a black woman with incredible skill, but due to her race and gender, there was nowhere for her to play professional baseball. It would take grit and persistence to fulfil her dream.

At age 15, Toni began playing for the Twin Cities Colored Giants, a semi-pro men's travelling team. Around 1946, she joined her sister in San Francisco, where she began playing amateur American Legion baseball. Soon she joined the San Francisco Sea Lions, and then the semi-pro Black Pelicans in New Orleans. In 1949, she was signed to a popular minor league team, the New Orleans Creoles. She played so well that she was featured in newspapers. In 1953, she became the first woman to play major league professional baseball, signing with a professional Negro League team, the Indianapolis Clowns.

After professional baseball integrated, the Major League teams started recruiting the best black players from the Negro Leagues – and ticket sales at Negro League games suffered. Although Toni was hired to draw crowds to Clowns games, she proved her worth with her skill. She played second base and batted a .243 average. She ran fast: 100 yards in 11 seconds.

Despite her success, Toni still dealt with sexism throughout her career. She was often benched, and teammates said things like, 'Go home and fix your husband some biscuits.' But in 1990, she was featured in exhibits at the Baseball Hall of Fame. She will always be remembered for breaking the gender line in baseball.

**...HAS A BASEBALL FIELD NAMED IN HER HONOUR IN ST PAUL, MINNESOTA.**

**...WAS A NURSE AFTER HER RETIREMENT, BUT OFTEN PLAYED BASEBALL FOR FUN.**

**HER TALENT AS A KID MADE THE MANAGER OF THE ST LOUIS SAINTS INCLUDE HER IN HIS ALL-BOYS BASEBALL CAMP.**

**WOAH!**

**ONLY MEMBER OF THE CLOWNS TO GET A HIT OFF OF THE FAMOUS PITCHER SATCHEL PAIGE AT AN EXHIBITION GAME.**

FIRST AFRICAN AMERICAN TO WIN A GRAND SLAM TITLE.

FIRST AFRICAN AMERICAN TO PLAY IN A US NATIONAL TENNIS COMPETITION.

IN THE INTERNATIONAL TENNIS HALL OF FAME.

'IN THE FIELD OF SPORTS YOU ARE MORE OR LESS ACCEPTED FOR WHAT YOU DO RATHER THAN WHAT YOU ARE.' — ALTHEA GIBSON

# ALTHEA GIBSON

## TENNIS PLAYER

Althea Gibson was born in 1927 and grew up in New York City, USA. She was a wild child, often skipping school, but one day she stumbled upon a community-designated 'play street' filled with kids playing sport. Sport gave her a sense of self-worth, and she threw herself into the games. At 13, she was invited to play at a top New York all-black tennis club. Within a year, in 1941, Althea won her first American Tennis Association tournament. In 1944 and 1945, she won the girls' division national title. Civil rights activists Dr Robert W. Johnson and Dr Hubert A. Eaton Junior saw Althea's potential to be like baseball player Jackie Robinson and use her talents to cross the racial divide in sport. They invited her to live with their families and sponsored her tennis career and education.

Althea wanted to play in the US Lawn Tennis Association (USLTA) tournaments, but most USLTA facilities were still restricted to white people. Alice Marble, a world-famous white tennis champion, wrote a scathing article about racism in tennis. In 1950, Althea was finally allowed to compete at the prestigious US National Championship at Forest Hills, becoming the first person of colour to play on their courts. Although she did not win, she gained international attention.

In 1951, she was invited to play at Wimbledon, making her the first black person to cross the colour line in international tennis. At the 1956 French Open, she became the first black player to win a Grand Slam title, and she met a new doubles partner and lifelong friend, Angela Buxton. Together they won many tournaments, including the Wimbledon doubles and French Open doubles. In 1957 and 1958, Althea was the champion at both Wimbledon and the US Nationals, proving she was a force in the tennis world! She won an impressive 11 national and international titles.

After ending her professional tennis career, Althea spent the rest of her life making public appearances, teaching, playing sport and giving back to the community. This tennis legend helped to convince people of the importance of desegregation and paved the way for many athletes of colour to follow their dreams.

#1 NAMED FEMALE ATHLETE OF THE YEAR BY THE AP IN 1957 AND '58.

FIRST BLACK WOMAN TO APPEAR ON THE COVERS OF *SPORTS ILLUSTRATED* AND *TIME* MAGAZINES.

AWARDED THE 1957 WIMBLEDON TROPHY BY THE QUEEN!

FIRST AFRICAN AMERICAN TO PLAY GOLF IN THE LPGA IN 1964.

CO-FOUNDED THE ALTHEA GIBSON FOUNDATION, WHICH HELPS UNDERPRIVILEGED KIDS LEARN TO PLAY GOLF AND TENNIS AND EARN SCHOLARSHIPS.

WON TOURNAMENTS ALL OVER THE WORLD, INCLUDING IN ASIA, AUSTRALIA, ITALY, WALES AND AT THE PAN AMERICAN GAMES.

THE ORIGINAL BAD GIRL OF ROLLER DERBY.

HELPED TO PIONEER THE LOOK AND ATTITUDE OF ROLLER DERBY.

INDUCTED INTO THE NATIONAL ROLLER DERBY HALL OF FAME.

'WHAT THE KIDS ARE DOING NOW WITH PUNK ROCK I DID 30 YEARS AGO.' — ANN CALVELLO

# ANN CALVELLO

## ROLLER DERBY

'Banana Nose', 'Meanest Mama on Skates' and 'The Lioness' were all nicknames for the bad girl of roller derby, Ann Calvello. She didn't want to look like the other tanned, blonde girls on skates. Way before punk rock style was in fashion, Ann created her own look with crazy colourful hair, clothes and make-up. She knew how to intimidate and was all aggression on the track, playing the villain to stir up the crowd and boost ticket sales.

Ann Theresa Calvello was born in Rhode Island, USA in 1929. Her family moved to San Francisco in 1941, and she roller-skated all over the old streets of the city. Roller derby was also born from the Great Depression — in the 1930s, endurance activities from dancing marathons to cycling marathons were popular forms of entertainment. In 1935, the first roller derby was organised, with 25 teams of men and women skating around an arena — the first team to reach 3,000 miles (4,828 km) won. This evolved into a two-team, physical contact sport where teams scored points by passing one another around the rink. Pushing and shoving were encouraged, but Ann helped shape it into the sport we know today: a fast-paced competition with the flair and attitude of pro wrestling.

At 18, Ann joined a travelling all-girl roller derby team and toured Europe. In the 50s and 60s, she played on many teams, including the San Francisco Bay Bombers and the Jersey Jolters. Ann would sneak up on players, trash talk and get into scrapes, playing the part of the rabble-rouser, riling up the crowd. The game was also an intense physical contact sport, and Ann was a fierce competitor who endured cracked ribs and broken bones from hard landings and intense plays.

Ann skated in every era of roller derby from the 40s to the 2000s. Even at age 71 she continued to compete. She will always be remembered as a Queen of Roller Derby.

NICKNAMED 'BANANA NOSE' BECAUSE SHE BROKE HER NOSE 12 TIMES IN THE RINK.

APRIL 15, 1972 WAS MADE ANN CALVELLO DAY IN INDIANAPOLIS.

THE DOCUMENTARY OF HER LIFE IS CALLED DEMON OF THE DERBY (2001).

HER ASTROLOGICAL SIGN WAS LEO; AS 'THE LIONESS' SHE WORE LION RINGS AND HAD EIGHT LION TATTOOS.

OFTEN PLAYED THE VILLAINESS OPPOSITE GOOD-GIRL JOANIE WESTON, AKA THE BLONDE BOMBER.

FAMOUSLY QUIPPED

JOE NAMATH IS THE ANN CALVELLO OF FOOTBALL.

FIRST WOMAN TO RIDE 40KM IN LESS THAN AN HOUR IN 1963.

STILL HOLDS THE WOMEN'S WORLD RECORD AT 446 KM BIKED IN 12 HOURS.

BEST BRITISH ALL-AROUND CYCLIST FOR 25 YEARS STRAIGHT.

'[SHE] JUST HAD HER OWN IDEAS OF WHAT SHE WAS GOING TO DO, AND SHE DID IT. NOTHING STOOD IN HER WAY.' - DENISE BURTON-COLE, CHAMPION CYCLIST AND BERYL'S DAUGHTER

# BERYL BURTON

## CYCLIST

Beryl Burton is one of the greatest cyclists in history. She dominated the sport for 25 years as the British Best All-Rounder. She won seven world titles and 96 titles in her native UK. She paid her own way and, as a woman, received little recognition from the British public and press. But she didn't care; she was dedicated to being the best in the sport she loved.

Beryl Charnock was born in West Yorkshire in 1937. As a teenager she worked at a tailoring firm, where she met Charlie Burton, who introduced her to cycling. She married him at 17, and he supported her throughout her cycling career by serving as her bike mechanic and caring for their daughter.

Beryl started competing in the British Best All-Rounder annual cycling time trials, in which a cyclist had a certain amount of time to bike as far as possible. In 1959, Beryl won it for the first time, and she won every year until 1983. She was Britain's fastest woman.

In 1967, Beryl did the unthinkable: she broke a men's speed record. During a 12-hour time trial, Beryl closed in on Mike McNamara, who was about to break the world record. But Beryl was too quick. She casually offered him a sweet as she passed him, then pushed on to set the new world record, biking 446 km. Her record stood as the fastest for both male and female cyclists for two years, and is still the women's distance record today.

In 1968, Beryl cycled 100 miles (161 km) in 3 hours 55 minutes and 5 seconds, setting a new women's record. She kept setting new speed records for 10 miles (16 km), 25 miles (40 km), 30 miles (48 km) and 50 miles (80.5 km). Throughout her career, she also raced internationally, winning the UCI Road World Championship twice and the UCI Track Cycling World Championship five times.

Beryl won her last title in 1986 and continued to compete for the rest of her life. She actually died on her bicycle while riding in her neighbourhood, suffering a cardiac arrest in 1996. She is now remembered as one of the fastest women ever on two wheels.

HER DAUGHTER, DENISE, ALSO A CYCLIST, GREW UP TO BEAT BERYL IN A NATIONAL RACE.

WON A TOTAL OF 15 WORLD CHAMPIONSHIP MEDALS IN UCI ROAD CYCLING AND TRACK CYCLING.

WROTE AN AUTOBIOGRAPHY, PERSONAL BEST.

IT'S A GREAT WORKOUT!

EARNED MONEY BY WORKING ON HER FRIEND'S RHUBARB FARM.

AWARDED ORDER OF THE BRITISH EMPIRE HONOURS IN 1964 AND 1968.

THE OLYMPICS DID NOT HAVE WOMEN'S CYCLING UNTIL 1984.

FIRST WOMAN ADMITTED INTO THE UNITED STATES POLO ASSOCIATION.

DISGUISED HERSELF AS A MAN FOR 20 YEARS TO PLAY POLO.

HER DAUGHTER BECAME ONE OF THE TOP POLO PLAYERS IN THE WORLD.

'GOING DOWN THE FIELD WITH SEVEN HEAD OF HORSES BROADSIDE, GETTING BUMPED BY 900 POUNDS OF HORSE AND MAN, JUST HOLDING THAT LINE STEADY FOR TWO SECONDS TO MAKE THAT SHOT. GOD, I LOVE THAT GAME.' - SUE SALLY HALE

# SUE SALLY HALE

## POLO PLAYER

Sue Sally Hale prepared for polo by putting on a disguise. Binding her breasts, tucking away her long hair and applying a fake moustache, she became the mysterious Mr A. Jones, who always disappeared right after a game. The US Polo Association (USPA) barred women from playing professionally, but that didn't stop Sue Sally, even if it meant playing in drag.

Born in 1937, Sue Sally grew up in Los Angeles, USA, loving horses and polo. She would ride her pony near the Will Rogers Polo Club, and club founder Duke Coulter took her under his wing.

Sue Sally could play polo with the best of them, and her male teammates enjoyed having her on the field, but the USPA did not allow female players to compete. Her stepfather helped her create the perfect disguise, and for 20 years, from the 1950s to 1972, she played polo as a man. Her teammates kept her secret because she was such a valuable player. Out of disguise, at post-game parties she often heard opposing players discussing how well A. Jones had played.

In 1957, she started a riding school and joined the Carmel Valley Polo Club. Her old mentor Duke later invited her to play at his club, where she had learned polo. But she was forced to leave when visiting players refused to play against a woman. She was furious and began to fight back.

**NO GIRLS!**

Sue Sally started organising unofficial games at her club, and she began receiving recognition as herself. She lobbied, and when that didn't work, Sue Sally threatened them: if women could not play in tournaments, she would reveal that she'd fooled them for decades as A. Jones. That did it! In 1972, she and the club's other female players received their membership cards.

Sue Sally was one of the most influential people to play polo. Her actions made polo a co-ed sport.

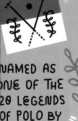

NAMED AS ONE OF THE 20 LEGENDS OF POLO BY THE POLO MAGAZINE.

CONTINUED TO PLAY DURING ALL 5 OF HER PREGNANCIES.

WROTE TO THE USPA FOR MEMBERSHIP EVERY YEAR FOR 20 YEARS.

WAS GIVEN A TWO-GOAL RANK BY THE USPA.

FINISHED A GAME WITH A BROKEN LEG.

**GENTLEMEN, BETTER BOYS THAN YOU HAVE TRIED. BE MY GUEST.**

RESPONDED TO MEN WHO THREATENED TO RUN HER OVER, MAKING THE 'BOYS' LOSE FOCUS ON THEIR GAME.

BECAME THE FIRST WOMAN TO CLIMB MT EVEREST IN 1975.

STARTED JAPAN'S FIRST WOMEN'S MOUNTAINEERING CLUB IN 1969.

FIRST WOMAN TO COMPLETE THE 'SEVEN SUMMITS.'

'AS LONG AS MY BODY IS ABLE, I'LL KEEP DOING WHAT I LOVE.' — JUNKO TABEI

# JUNKO TABEI

## MOUNTAINEER

In Japan in the 1960s and 1970s, opportunities for women outside of the home were very limited, with few options even for university-educated women. But Junko Tabei knew she had the potential to achieve extraordinary things. She would conquer the world's tallest peaks and become a role model for women everywhere.

Junko Tabei was born in 1939 and started climbing at age 10. She liked that climbing wasn't about speed or competition — it was about making your way to the top with your team. Junko continued to climb in high school, and after university joined predominantly male climbing clubs. Many men refused to climb with her, but she didn't care; she was too busy climbing some of Japan's tallest mountains.

CAMPAIGNED TO PROTECT EVEREST'S ECOSYSTEM FROM CLIMBERS' RUBBISH.

In 1969, Junko founded Japan's first women's mountaineering group, which she led up Annapurna III in 1970. After that victory, she set her sights on Mount Everest. The club scheduled a climb for 1975 and began looking for sponsors. Junko remembers being told that they 'should be raising children instead'. Many potential sponsors thought it was 'impossible' for women to climb Everest. Finally, a Japanese newspaper and Nihon Television funded their climb. She would lead 14 women up Earth's tallest mountain.

CRAWLED SIDEWAYS ON EVEREST'S ICY KNIFE-LIKE RIDGE 6,000 M IN THE AIR.

Mount Everest is one of the most prestigious and dangerous mountains to summit due to its extreme size, rough terrain and terrible weather. Many people have tried to climb Everest only to turn back or, worse, die on the mountain. Twelve days before summitting, Junko and her team were hit by an avalanche — she was buried under four members of her team and had to be dug out by a guide. Luckily no one died, but Junko was covered in painful bruises. Finally, on 16 May 1975, Junko became the first woman to summit Everest — and a role model to women worldwide.

DESCRIBED THE PEAK OF EVEREST AS 'SMALLER THAN A TATAMI MAT'.

In 1992, Junko achieved her next goal: to conquer the rest of the 'seven summits'—the tallest summit on each continent. Then she went on to try and scale the tallest mountain in each country in the world, checking 70 countries off her list. Junko proved countless times that women can achieve the 'impossible'.

36TH PERSON TO SUMMIT MT EVEREST.

THE KING OF NEPAL CONGRATULATED JUNKO AFTER SHE CLIMBED EVEREST.

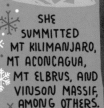

SHE SUMMITTED MT KILIMANJARO, MT ACONCAGUA, MT ELBRUS, AND VINSON MASSIF, AMONG OTHERS.

INDUCTED INTO THE OLYMPIC HALL OF FAME.

FIRST US WOMAN TO WIN THREE GOLD MEDALS FOR ATHLETICS DURING ONE OLYMPIC YEAR.

PIONEER FOR CIVIL RIGHTS.

USA

'MY LEGACY IS TO THE YOUTH OF AMERICA, TO LET THEM KNOW THEY CAN BE ANYTHING THEY WANT TO BE.' – WILMA RUDOLF

# WILMA RUDOLPH

## ATHLETICS SPRINTER

Wilma Glodean Rudolph was born in Tennessee, USA in 1940. When Wilma was four she contracted polio that painfully wasted the muscles in her left leg, and doctors said she would never walk again. Physical therapy was her only hope, but because of unjust segregation laws, Wilma was banned from the all-white hospitals near her home. So every week, Wilma's mum took her on a 50-mile (80 km) bus ride to Nashville to get the treatment she needed. Against the odds, by age nine Wilma could walk again! She became the star of her high school basketball team, but the racism she experienced in the segregated South made her angry. It fuelled her competitive spirit, and she started 'fighting back in a new way' by winning.

BACK OF THE BUS!

When Wilma was 15, pioneering coach Ed Temple recruited her for an athletics summer camp, and in 1956, at age 16, Wilma qualified for the Olympics. She helped her team win a bronze medal in the 400 m relay. Four years later, at the 1960 Olympics, Wilma twisted her ankle the day before her events. She ran through the pain, and, with a taped-up ankle, won gold in the 100 m dash, the 200 m dash and the 4x400 m relay. Wilma was the first American woman to win three athletics gold medals at one Olympic Games. She became an international sensation!

Wilma went on a world media tour, and her hometown of Clarksville, Tennessee wanted to honour her with a parade. But there was a catch: only white people would be allowed to attend. Wilma refused to participate unless the parade was desegregated. She turned it into the first integrated event in Clarksville — and for the rest of her life used her fame to advocate for civil rights.

Wilma retired from racing at age 22. She established the Wilma Rudolph Foundation, which helps young athletes from underserved communities follow their dreams. Wilma died at age 54 from cancer, but her dedication to sports and civil rights lives on.

NICKNAMED 'SKEETER' BECAUSE SHE BUZZED AROUND THE BASKETBALL COURT.

IN THE NATIONAL TRACK AND FIELD HALL OF FAME AND THE INTERNATIONAL WOMEN'S SPORTS HALL OF FAME.

ABC

WAS ALSO A SCHOOL TEACHER AND COACH AFTER HER RETIREMENT.

WENT TO TENNESSEE STATE UNIVERSITY AND RAN WITH THE TIGERBELLES ATHLETICS TEAM.

CALLED 'THE BLACK GAZELLE' AND 'THE BLACK PEARL' IN EUROPEAN NEWSPAPERS.

MET QUEEN ELIZABETH AND PRESIDENT KENNEDY ON HER PRESS TOUR.

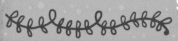

# MUSCLE ANATOMY

To get strong and healthy, a sporstwoman needs to understand how her body works. Our muscles let our bodies do what they need to do to win!

STERNOCLEIDOMASTOID

DELTOID

BICEP

BRACHIORADIALIS

WRIST FLEXORS

PECTORALS

BRACHIALIS

TRICEP

RECTUS ABDOMINIS

SERRATUS ANTERIOR

OBLIQUES

GLUTEALS

VASTUS LATERALIS

TIBIALIS ANTERIOR

QUADRICEPS

ABDUCTOR LONGUS

SOLEUS

GASTROCNEMIUS

VASTUS MEDIALIS

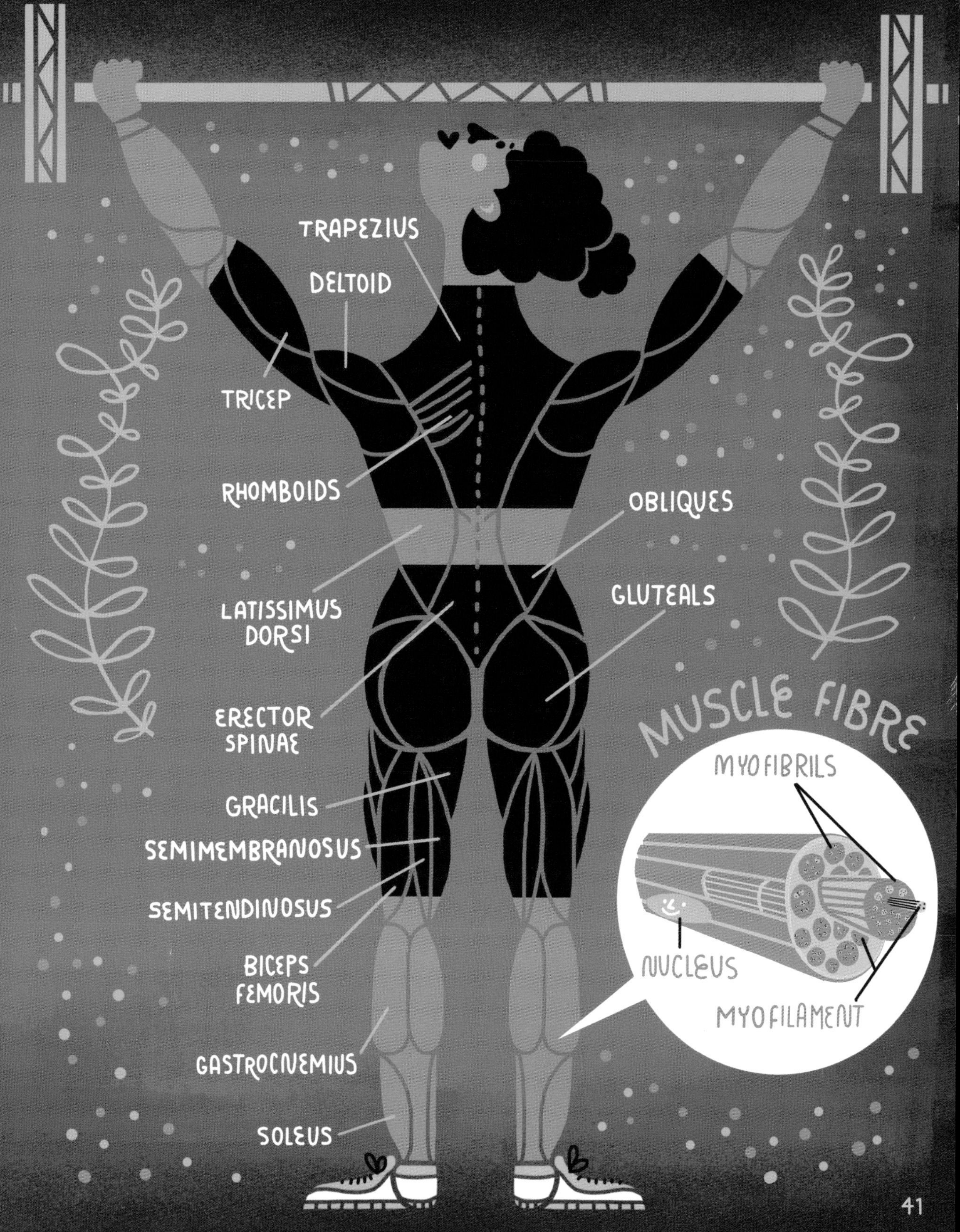

TRAPEZIUS

DELTOID

TRICEP

RHOMBOIDS

OBLIQUES

GLUTEALS

LATISSIMUS DORSI

ERECTOR SPINAE

GRACILIS

SEMIMEMBRANOSUS

SEMITENDINOSUS

BICEPS FEMORIS

GASTROCNEMIUS

SOLEUS

MUSCLE FIBRE

MYOFIBRILS

NUCLEUS

MYOFILAMENT

COACHED THE FIRST UNDEFEATED TEAM IN NCAA DIVISION I TO WIN THE NCAA NATIONAL.

ONE OF THE WINNINGEST COACHES IN COLLEGE BASKETBALL.

SECOND WOMAN AND FIRST FEMALE COACH IN THE NAISMITH HALL OF FAME.

'HARD LESSONS ARE SOMETIMES LEARNED THROUGH SPORTS. YOU HAVE TO BRING IT EVERY DAY. IF YOU DON'T BRING IT EVERY DAY, SOMETIMES IT DOESN'T WORK OUT FOR YOU.' —JODY CONRADT

# JODY CONRADT

## BASKETBALL COACH

Jody Conradt transformed women's basketball into the respected powerhouse sport it is today, and coached one of the winningest women's university teams in basketball history. When she started coaching, it was her unpaid side job, but by the time she retired in 2007, she was making over half a million dollars a year. When many thought female sport at university was a joke, she proved its worth with the sheer force of winning.

Born Addie Jo Conradt in Texas, USA in 1941, Jody always had state pride. She took up basketball in high school and dreamed of becoming a professional basketball star. She played while earning a degree in physical education from Baylor University. Jody graduated in 1963 and started teaching while coaching high school basketball. At first Jody coached the slow-paced six-player style of women's basketball, where only two players could run the entire length of the court. In 1969, Jody moved on to university basketball, and women started playing just like men did: five on five, with all the players running the full court. In 1973, she moved to the University of Texas, Arlington. The budget was only $1,200 for the entire women's sports programme, and Jody coached all three women's teams. With her in charge, the women's basketball, volleyball and softball teams all won state championships.

Jody was making a name for herself; she was recruited to coach the Longhorns women's basketball team at the University of Texas in Austin. She started on a salary of $19,000, which shocked critics and made the news. Under her coaching, the Lady Longhorns were unstoppable in the Southwest Conference and won 183 consecutive league games. In 1986, Jody led the Lady Longhorns to win their first national championship after an undefeated season. The next year she coached the US national team to win the Pan American Games. In 1997, she became the first female basketball coach to win 700 games.

Jody retired with 900 wins to her credit. She led a whole generation of female champions, and her influence changed the nation's perceptions of women's sport.

NAMED WBCA NATIONAL COACH OF THE YEAR IN 1984 AND 1986.

RECEIVED A LIFETIME ACHIEVEMENT AWARD IN 2010 FROM THE NACWAA.

TIME TO STUDY!

99 PER CENT OF HER PLAYERS GRADUATED FROM UNIVERSITY.

COACHED ONE OF THE FIRST WOMEN'S TEAMS TO BE RECOGNISED BY THE NCAA.

WORKED AS THE WOMEN'S ATHLETIC DIRECTOR AT THE UNIVERSITY OF TEXAS STARTING IN 1992.

FINAL FOUR

MADE IT TO THE FINAL FOUR TWICE.

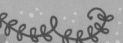

AWARDED THE PRESIDENTIAL MEDAL OF FREEDOM FOR HER CAREER AND WORK TOWARD GENDER EQUALITY AND LGBT RIGHTS.

CONSIDERED ONE OF THE GREATEST TENNIS PLAYERS OF ALL TIME.

STARTED THE FIRST WOMEN'S PRO TENNIS TOURNAMENT.

FIRST WOMAN TO BE NAMED SPORTS ILLUSTRATED SPORTSPERSON OF THE YEAR.

'EVERY ONE OF US IS AN INDIVIDUAL, A HUMAN BEING WITH A BEATING HEART, WHO CARES AND WANTS TO LIVE THEIR AUTHENTIC LIFE.' — BILLIE JEAN KING

# BILLIE JEAN KING

## TENNIS PLAYER

Billie Jean King (née Moffitt) was born in 1943 in California, USA. At age 12, she fell in love with tennis, but not with the sport's elitism. To play tennis back then, you needed to join an expensive club, many of which had racist policies and sexist attitudes. Billie Jean would become one of the best players in history and use her power to change tennis forever. In 1961, aged 17, Billie Jean shocked everyone when she won the doubles at Wimbledon. In 1966, she won the Wimbledon singles for the first time. From then she dominated singles and doubles tournaments all over the world.

In 1968, the United States Tennis Association (USTA) began to award prize money for their events. Men's prizes were worth over twice as much as women's. When Billie Jean won Wimbledon in 1968, she received only £750; the male champion won £2,000. So, with eight others, she started her own pro women's tour, the Virginia Slims. By 1971, they secured $10,000 in prize money for each event. Billie Jean dominated the Slims tour and became the first female athlete to win $100,000 in one year. In 1972, she was the first woman to be named *Sports Illustrated* Sportsperson of the Year.

In 1973, the USTA finally decided to award men and women equal prize money. The feminist movement was in full swing, with women demanding equal treatment and pay. Many people were still sceptical about about the value of women in sport. One outspoken critic was Bobby Riggs, a former men's tennis champion, who challenged Billie Jean to a 'battle of the sexes'. At first she declined, but then Grand Slam winner Margaret Court lost to him. Billie Jean realised that she had to beat Bobby so the world would see the value of women's tennis. She crushed him, winning 6-4, 6-3, 6-3. Her win led to the creation of the Women's Tennis Association.

Billie Jean retired in 1983 with a total of 39 Grand Slam titles. Today she continues to fight for equal treatment for women in sport and the workforce.

CAME OUT IN 1981, BECOMING THE FIRST OPENLY LESBIAN SUPERSTAR ATHLETE.

THE BILLIE JEAN KING LEADERSHIP INITIATIVE WORKS TOWARD MORE DIVERSITY IN THE WORK-FORCE AND LEADERSHIP.

COACHED THE 1996 US OLYMPIC TENNIS TEAM.

NAMED ONE OF *LIFE* MAGAZINE'S '100 MOST IMPORTANT AMERICANS OF THE 20TH CENTURY'.

FOUNDED THE WOMEN'S SPORTS FOUNDATION IN 1974.

CHAUVINIST PIG!

GAVE BOBBY RIGGS A PIGLET BEFORE THE 'BATTLE OF THE SEXES' MATCH.

FIRST WOMAN INDUCTED INTO THE SKATEBOARDING HALL OF FAME IN 2010.

FIRST PROFESSIONAL FEMALE SKATEBOARDER.

FEATURED ON THE COVER OF LIFE MAGAZINE.

'A 53-YEAR SPAN IN SKATING, AND SO MANY THINK IT IS NEW FOR THE GIRLS. WHO WOULD HAVE THOUGHT IT WOULD GROW TO WHAT IT IS TODAY?' —PATTI McGEE

# PATTI McGEE

## SKATEBOARDER

In 1965, *Life* magazine described the skateboard as 'the most exhilarating and dangerous joyriding device this side of the hot rod'. So you can imagine how impressive a petite blonde girl doing a handstand on her skateboard looked on the cover of *Life*'s May 1965 issue. This was one of many of Patti McGee's public appearances throughout her skateboarding career, and she became one of the most influential skaters in history.

Patti was born in 1945 and grew up in Santa Monica, California, USA. She loved the ocean and surfing, but what does a surfer do when the surf is too low? Ride the road, of course! In 1962, Patti started skateboarding. She and her surfing friends would skateboard down hills and sneak into parking garages to practise tricks. Patti was a daredevil and would do handstands, figure of eights and 360s on her board. She also had a need for speed, and in 1965 became the fastest person on a skateboard after being pulled along by a motorcycle. That same year she became the female US National Skateboard Champion.

After her big win came opportunities. By age 19, she had become the first female professional skateboarder, sponsored by Hobie Skateboards. She travelled the country showing off her skills and teaching others. She appeared on TV and became the first woman on the cover of *Skateboarder* magazine. All of this helped make skateboarding a national sensation, and she was one of the most recognised people in the sport.

When skateboarding's popularity died down in the 1970s, Patti switched gears. She started skiing in Northern California; became a turquoise miner in Nevada; then worked as a leather smith! Patti settled down and ran a trading post in Arizona, where she raised her two children.

After 15 years there, Patti switched back into skateboarding. She started First Betty, now called the Original Betty Skateboard Company, which makes boards and sponsors female skaters. Pioneer Patti can still be seen skating it up at local parks.

DID STUNTS FOR BEACH-PARTY MOVIES IN THE 1960s.

EARNED $250 A MONTH WHEN SHE WENT PRO.

'SKATE BETTY' IS SLANG FOR A GIRL SKATER.

HER BROTHER BUILT HER FIRST SKATEBOARD OUT OF WOOD AND ROLLER-SKATE WHEELS.

WAS IN A COMMERCIAL FOR BELL TELEPHONE.

INDUCTED INTO THE MALIBU SURF LEGENDS IN 2004.

NAMED ALL-AMERICAN IN VOLLEYBALL 3 TIMES.

CONSIDERED ONE OF THE GREATEST VOLLEYBALL PLAYERS IN US HISTORY.

CAPTAIN OF THE US VOLLEYBALL TEAM AND WON A SILVER MEDAL AT THE 1984 OLYMPICS.

FLO HYMAN MEMORIAL AWARD WAS GIVEN TO ATHLETES WHO EMBODIED FLO'S 'DIGNITY, SPIRIT, AND COMMITMENT TO EXCELLENCE'.

'IT'S A MATTER OF ACHIEVEMENT, A MATTER OF ACCOMPLISHMENT, A MATTER OF SOMETHING WELL DONE. AND THAT'S WHEN YOU GET PERSONAL SATISFACTION.' — FLO HYMAN

# FLO HYMAN

## VOLLEYBALL PLAYER

WHIPPER-SNAPPER!

Women's volleyball in the 1960s was seen as a hobby, not a serious sport. At the time, people considered volleyball largely for white people and basketball mostly for black people, so Flo Hyman — a black woman — did not fit the stereotype of a volleyball player. But her skills changed how Americans viewed the sport. She would be recognised as one of the greatest players in the world.

Flora Jean 'Flo' Hyman was born in 1954 in California, USA. She grew tall quickly — by age 17 she was six feet five inches. Her strength and height made her powerful at serving and spiking the ball. She worked hard to perfect her technique, but she had more than athletic talent. Flo enjoyed the teamwork of volleyball and had leadership qualities and a great attitude. She always put her team's success before her own ego. While playing for the University of Houston, she was named All-American three times. In 1975, Flo joined the US women's national team.

The US women's volleyball team needed a lot of preparation to be ready to compete in the Olympics. Despite year-round training, the team didn't even qualify for the 1976 Games. Flo was instrumental in pushing her teammates to be their best, and all their hard work paid off: they qualified for the 1980 Olympics. But due to Cold War conflicts, the US boycotted the Games, and none of the US teams could compete.

Flo and her teammates kept working and were ready for the 1984 Olympics, where she led her team to a silver medal. Her family cried when she didn't win the gold, but for Flo, even competing was a dream come true. She thought about how far her team had come and was proud of her fellow players.

In 1986, while playing volleyball in Japan, Flo died suddenly. In her memory, the Flo Hyman Memorial Award was given to 18 outstanding female athletes from 1987 to 2004.

NAMED 'BEST ATTACKER' AT THE 1981 WORLD CUP.

COMPETED IN THE WORLD CUP, THE PAN AMERICAN GAMES AND THE WORLD UNIVERSITY GAMES.

HER BROTHER'S LIFE WAS SAVED BY GETTING CHECKED FOR MARFAN SYNDROME AFTER FLO'S DEATH.

NICKNAMED HERSELF THE 'OLD LADY' ON THE TEAM.

LOBBIED FOR MORE MONEY FOR WOMEN'S SPORTS IN THE US.

THE US VOLLEYBALL TEAM COACH, ARIE SELINGER, TAUGHT HER TO NOT BE AFRAID TO 'HIT THE FLOOR'.

FIRST PERSON TO WIN THE IDITAROD 3 YEARS IN A ROW, AND FIRST WOMAN TO WIN IT 4 TIMES.

HELD THE IDITAROD SPEED RECORD FROM 1986 TO 1992.

HER YEAR-ROUND DOG-CARE TECHNIQUES BECAME THE NEW STANDARD PRACTICE.

'THERE ARE MANY HARD THINGS IN LIFE, BUT THERE'S ONLY ONE SAD THING, AND THAT IS GIVING UP.' – SUSAN BUTCHER

# SUSAN BUTCHER

## DOG MUSHER

The Iditarod is considered the 'Last Great Race on Earth'. For over 1,688 km, mushers need to face sub-zero temperatures, wild animals, frozen rivers and the perilous Alaskan wilderness. A musher must be strong enough to push the sled and have the mental and physical endurance for the long race. Susan Butcher wanted to be the greatest dog musher that ever lived.

Susan Howlet Butcher was born in 1954 and grew up in Massachusetts, USA. When her mum gave her a Siberian husky, Susan found her calling. After high school she relocated to Colorado and began training sled dogs. She then moved again to Alaska and started training for the Iditarod. Searching for a dog team, she got some race-ready huskies from a kennel owner in exchange for training his younger dogs. She placed 19th in the 1978 Iditarod — the first woman to finish 'in the money'.

Racing was very dangerous, and each time Susan set out on the Iditarod, she faced new challenges. In the 1982 race she crashed into a tree, then got stuck in a snowstorm, but still finished second. In the 1984 race, a frozen river gave way under her sled; she nearly drowned, but her dogs pulled her to safety. Again she came second. In 1985, Susan had to fight off an angry moose with an axe; the moose killed two and injured 13 of her dogs, and she was out of the race. Another woman, Libby Riddles, became the first woman to win the Iditarod that year. Susan continued to push herself despite these setbacks.

In 1986, Susan finally won her first Iditarod, setting a new speed record. She won twice more, becoming the first person to win the Iditarod three years in a row. In 1990, she won again, finishing hours before her competitors and setting a new speed record for the race: 11 days, 1 hour, 53 minutes and 23 seconds.

In dog sledding, men and women compete against each other. Susan is remembered as one of the sport's first top athletes.

FINISHED IN THE TOP 5 IN 12 OF HER 17 IDITAROD RACES.

WON FEMALE ATHLETE OF THE YEAR 2 YEARS IN A ROW.

IN 1979, BECAME THE FIRST WOMAN TO LEAD A DOG TEAM UP MOUNT MCKINLEY.

FOUNDED TRAIL BREAKERS KENNEL WITH HER HUSBAND, WHO IS ALSO A DOG MUSHER.

THE IDITAROD IS BASED ON THE SUPPLY ROUTES FOR MINING TOWNS FROM THE 19TH AND EARLY 20TH CENTURIES.

CALLED THE 'STRONGEST WOMAN IN HISTORY'.

WON GOLD MEDALS 6 TIMES AT THE INTERNATIONAL POWERLIFTING FEDERATION CHAMPIONSHIPS.

SET THE WORLD RECORD FOR WOMEN'S BENCH PRESS AT 152 KG.

'TO GET WOMEN STRONG IS VERY EMPOWERING...IT IS NICE NOT TO BE HELPLESS.' — BEV FRANCIS

# BEV FRANCIS

## WEIGHTLIFTER AND BODYBUILDER

Beverley Francis was born in Australia in 1955. She always admired strength and was fascinated with muscles. In a world where women were expected to be weak and small, she wanted to become strong, large and independent. As a teen, Bev was a shot putter, and in 1974 she started weight-training seriously.

Bodybuilding requires intense discipline and focus. It's not just about lifting weights; it is about sculpting the body. It is twice as hard for women to retain muscle, so Bev trained more than anyone else. With such dedication she was undefeated in every powerlifting competition she entered, and she was the World Powerlifting Champion six times from 1980 to 1985. During this time, she broke over 40 world powerlifting records, including becoming the first woman to bench-press over 136 kg.

Bev was strong, but the International Federation of Bodybuilding (IFBB) Ms Olympia competition was not just about strength. Bodybuilding championships focus mainly on the symmetry and definition of the muscles, but female bodybuilders were also judged on their femininity. Bev sparked a national conversation about how muscles should be a larger part of female bodybuilding when she was featured in the movie *Pumping Iron II* in 1983 and again when she placed 10th in the 1986 Ms Olympia competition. She thought they should have ranked her either first or last based on her body. Bev kept competing, coming third in 1987, '88 and '89, and second in 1990.

When Bev took the Ms Olympia stage in 1991, the crowd gasped and cheered in awe. Her physique could beat most male middleweight bodybuilders. She was in the lead in all the categories but still came in second, losing by only one point. Despite the loss, she was recognised as the most muscular woman the world had ever seen. Again she helped to change the conversation about how to evaluate female strength.

Bev went on to start Powerhouse Gym in New York City. She continues to train and empower other women to get strong.

WON FIRST PLACE IN THE 1987 IFBB WORLD PROFESSIONAL BODYBUILDING CHAMPIONSHIP.

EARNED A DEGREE IN PHYSICAL EDUCATION FROM THE UNIVERSITY OF MELBOURNE IN 1976.

WAS OFTEN TREATED LIKE A FREAK BECAUSE OF HER MUSCLES, BUT SHE NEVER LET OTHERS' OPINIONS STOP HER.

WAS ON THE AUSTRALIAN TRACK AND FIELD TEAM AS A SHOT PUTTER FROM 1977 TO 1982 (EXCEPT 1980).

HER BEST LIFTS INCLUDE SQUATTING 227 KG, BENCH-PRESSING 152 KG, AND A DEAD LIFT OF 227 KG.

MET HER HUSBAND DURING THE MAKING OF *PUMPING IRON II*.

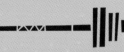

FIRST GYMNAST IN HISTORY TO BE AWARDED A SCORE OF A PERFECT 10.0

FIRST IN THE INTERNATIONAL GYMNASTICS HALL OF FAME.

FIRST PERSON FROM ROMANIA TO WIN A GOLD MEDAL IN THE OLYMPICS.

'EVERYBODY WAS SURPRISED TO SEE A 14-YEAR-OLD BEING ABLE TO DO THE LEVEL OF GYMNASTICS THAT I DID, BUT EVEN I DIDN'T KNOW THAT I WAS EXTRAORDINARY AT THE TIME.' — NADIA COMĂNECI

# NADIA COMĂNECI

## GYMNAST

Nadia Comăneci's performance at the 1976 Olympic Games epitomised flawlessness. With grace and ease, this 14-year-old girl swung through her uneven bars routine and earned a perfect score of 10.0. This achievement was assumed to be so unattainable that the Olympic scoreboards were not even equipped to display it. Nadia gave six more perfect performances, and with seven scores of 10.0, she made Olympic history.

Nadia was born in 1961 in a small town in Romania, then a Soviet-influenced state where national pride was big business for the government. Her gymnastic training started at age six, with all her coaching paid for by Romania. At a boarding school run by her famed coach, Béla Károlyi, the training was intense, but by age 13 she was ready to compete internationally.

In 1975, she was the youngest person ever to compete at the 'Champions All' tournament. That year she earned four gold and one silver medal at the European Championships. In 1976, she showed the world gymnastic perfection at the Olympics, winning gold in the uneven bars, balance beam and individual all-around. She also won a silver in the team all-around and a bronze on the floor. Nadia returned to Romania as a 'Hero of Socialist Labour'. She defended her European Championship title in 1977 and won two gold and two silver medals in the 1980 Moscow Olympics.

Although Nadia was a celebrity, her treatment in Romania was anything but glamorous. In 1981, Béla Károlyi defected to the United States. The government, afraid that Nadia would also defect, restricted her travel and had police follow her. Nadia said, 'I started to feel like a prisoner. In reality, I'd always been one.' She retired from gymnastics in 1984, and in 1989 Nadia escaped from Romania by walking through the forest into Hungary. She made her way to New York, where she was given asylum.

Nadia's performance in the 1976 Olympics showed the world what is possible in gymnastics. Now Nadia fundraises for many charities and her academy trains future generations of gymnasts.

CHOSEN TO REPRESENT HER COUNTRY IN GYMNASTICS AT AGE 6 WHEN SHE WAS SPOTTED DOING CARTWHEELS AT SCHOOL.

RECIPIENT OF THE FLO HYMAN AWARD.

HELPS TO RUN THE ART CONNER GYMNASTICS ACADEMY AND THE BART & NADIA SPORTS EXPERIENCE.

STILL HOLDS THE RECORD FOR THE MOST 10.0s SCORED DURING AN OLYMPIC GAMES.

WON HER FIRST NATIONAL JUNIOR CHAMPIONSHIP AT 9 YEARS OLD.

THE ONLY PERSON TO RECEIVE THE OLYMPIC ORDER TWICE.

SET A WORLD RECORD IN THE HEPTATHLON.

NAMED SPORTSWOMAN OF THE YEAR IN 1986 BY THE OLYMPIC COMMITTEE.

VOTED THE GREATEST FEMALE ATHLETE OF THE 20TH CENTURY BY SPORTS ILLUSTRATED.

HAS WON 6 OLYMPIC MEDALS.

'I DON'T THINK BEING AN ATHLETE IS UNFEMININE;
I THINK OF IT AS A KIND OF GRACE.'

# JACKIE JOYNER-KERSEE

## HEPTATHLETE

**WON THE JESSE OWENS MEMORIAL MEDAL TWICE.**

**MARRIED HER COACH, BOB KERSEE, IN 1986.**

**HER BROTHER ALSO WON AN OLYMPIC GOLD MEDAL IN 1984.**

Jacqueline 'Jackie' Joyner was born in 1962 and grew up in East Saint Louis, USA. Work was scarce, and Jackie's family often lacked money for food, but her parents made sure their kids never got into trouble and they stressed the importance of education. After school, Jackie played basketball and volleyball at her local community centre and discovered athletics.

In high school she was in the athletics team and starred on their state championship basketball team. Jackie graduated with an impressive grade point average and a basketball scholarship to UCLA. At university, she played basketball but longed to be on the athletics team. She went to trials, but did not impress the coaches. Determined, she practised the long jump by herself until coach Bob Kersee noticed her passion. Together they trained in the seven heptathlon events: the 100 m hurdles, high jump, shot put, 200 m dash, long jump, javelin and 800 m run.

In 1981, Jackie's mother died, and Jackie began suffering from extreme exercise-induced asthma. Despite her grief and medical difficulty, she kept training. She won the heptathlon at the NCAA championship and the USA National Championship. But at the 1984 Olympics, her long jump performance fell short. She won the silver medal in the heptathlon — and was determined to win gold next time.

At the 1986 Goodwill Games (an alternative to the Olympics), Jackie broke the world record for the heptathlon; her score of 7,148 points made her the first person to score over 7,000. At the 1988 Olympics, Jackie won gold medals in the heptathlon and the long jump. She beat her own world record, with a score of 7,291, and her long jump of 7.4 m set an Olympic record. Jackie continued to win Olympic medals — a gold and a bronze in 1992 and a bronze in 1996 — making her one of the most decorated athletics competitors ever. Her world record still stands. After 18 years of competing, Jackie retired and is now recognised as one of the greatest athletes of all time.

**WON WORLD CHAMPIONSHIP GOLD MEDALS FOR HEPTATHLON IN 1987 AND FOR LONG JUMP IN 1987, '91 AND '93.**

**SHE WAS NAMED AFTER JACQUELINE KENNEDY BECAUSE HER GRANDMA KNEW SHE 'WOULD BE THE FIRST LADY OF SOMETHING'.**

FIRST FEMALE SKATER TO BREAK THE 39-SECOND BARRIER IN THE 500 M SPRINT.

WON 5 GOLD OLYMPIC MEDALS AND 1 BRONZE.

ONE OF THE MOST DECORATED ATHLETES IN OLYMPIC HISTORY.

IN THE US OLYMPIC HALL OF FAME.

'IF I PUT IN THE PHYSICAL WORK AND MY COMPETITOR DOES THE SAME KIND OF TRAINING, BUT DOESN'T HAVE THE STRONG POSITIVE MENTAL OUTLOOK THAT I DO, THEN SHE'S GOING TO BE BEATEN.' - BONNIE BLAIR

# BONNIE BLAIR

## SPEED-SKATER

Bonnie Kathleen Blair has been-ice skating since before she can remember. She was born in 1964 in New York, USA, into a family of avid skaters. Her parents took her out on the ice before she was two, and by four, Bonnie was already speed-skating. They moved to Illinois, where Bonnie won her first state competition aged seven.

At five foot five and 59 kg, Bonnie was considered very small for a speed-skater. She would have to rely on self-determination and technique to win. In 1984, she qualified for her first Olympics but lacked the money for training or travel. Since Bonnie was known in her hometown for her amazing positive attitude and kindness, the local police department raised $7,000 for Bonnie to compete. Bonnie went on to skate in three more Olympic Games, and her friends and family always showed up to cheer her on.

Bonnie won no medals in 1984, so she stepped up her efforts, weight-training to gain strength. At the 1988 Calgary Olympics, Bonnie won her first gold medal and set a new speed record for the 500 m: 39.10 seconds. She also won bronze in the 1,000 m.

At the 1992 Winter Olympics, with family and friends in the crowd waving flags, she won golds in the 500 m and 1,000 m. She did it again at the 1994 Winter Olympics, where she not only won gold in those same two events, but also won the 1,000 m by the largest margin ever. Her fans went wild, and she became the most decorated American in the history of the Winter Olympics!

She made history again in 1994 by breaking the 39-second barrier in speed-skating, setting a new record for the 500 m at 38.99 seconds. The next year, she bested her own score at 38.69 seconds, another world record.

Throughout her career, Bonnie relied on her own positive attitude and support from her community. She retired at age 31, a skating legend. She now runs the Bonnie Blair Charitable Fund and travels the United States, coaching and speaking.

HER LAST RACE WAS THE 1,000 M, WHERE SHE SET A NATIONAL RECORD AT MINUTE AND .05 SECONDS.

YAY!

HER BIRTH WAS ANNOUNCED OVER THE PA SYSTEM AT THE ICE RINK WHERE HER DAD AND SIBLINGS WERE SKATING.

BONNIE! U.S.A.

HER FRIENDS AND FAMILY IN THE STANDS WERE NICKNAMED THE 'BLAIR BUNCH'.

WON THE JAMES E. SULLIVAN AWARD AS TOP US AMATEUR ATHLETE IN 1992.

THE FIRST AMERICAN WOMAN TO WIN 5 OLYMPIC GOLD MEDALS.

FIRST FEMALE NBA REFEREE

HAS OFFICIATED NBA PLAYOFF GAMES AND THE NBA FINALS.

HAS REFEREED 2 WOMEN'S NATIONAL CHAMPIONSHIPS

'I REALLY BELIEVE THAT IF YOU REALLY ENJOY WHAT YOU'RE DOING, IT'S NOT WORK. I GO TO WORK EVERY DAY AND IT'S NOT WORK FOR ME' –VIOLET PALMER

# VIOLET PALMER

## REFEREE

Violet Renice Palmer was born in 1964 and grew up in Los Angeles, USA. Her skill at high school basketball earned her a full scholarship to California State Polytechnic University, Pomona, where her team won two championships. In the summer she did scorekeeping and substitute refereeing for men's games — her first taste of officiating basketball.

Soon she was officiating university women's Division I games, where she worked all the important televised games. In 1995, the National Basketball Association (NBA) offered her a spot in their referee-training programme. She knew that moving to the NBA as a female ref meant she would have to prove her worth all over again. Many worried that the game was too rough and the language too foul for a woman ref to handle. NBA games were fast-paced and intense; there were fights. A ref needs to be right in the action, often taking a stray punch or an elbow to the face, all while being observant and on point about the rules.

Violet had a challenge: to convince the NBA's players and fans not to judge her based on her gender. She started refereeing pre-season NBA games and exhibitions. After two years she was promoted, and in 1997, she became the first woman to officiate a regular season NBA game. As she recalls, 'I didn't just kick the door — I knocked it down.'

With the world watching, many — coaches, players, reporters and other refs — were waiting for Violet to fail. Commentators told her to 'Go back to reffing women's games!' or 'Go back to the kitchen!' Violet ignored them and was a strong voice on the court, keeping up with the players and breaking up fights immediately. With guts, she showed the world that she belonged.

In 2006, Violet was the first woman to officiate an NBA playoff game, a job reserved for the best of the best. She went on to ref the 2009 NBA finals and the 2014 NBA all-star game. She retired as one of the most respected voices on the court.

DEE KANTNER WAS THE OTHER FEMALE REFEREE WORKING WITH HER IN 1997.

OFFICIATED 5 NCAA WOMEN'S FINAL FOURS.

MARRIED HER LONGTIME GIRLFRIEND IN 2014.

PLAYED POINT GUARD IN HIGH SCHOOL AND COLLEGE.

SHE TRIPPED AND TORE HER SHOULDER DURING A GAME AND WENT ON TO OFFICIATE THE WHOLE GAME USING ONLY ONE ARM WITHOUT A BREAK.

SHE HAS WON 5 GOLD, 4 SILVER AND 3 BRONZE MEDALS AT WORLD CHAMPIONSHIPS OVER HER CAREER.

IS ON THE BOARD FOR THE LONDON MARATHON AND THE SPORTS AID FOUNDATION.

HAS WON 11 GOLD, 4 SILVER AND 1 BRONZE PARALYMPIC MEDALS.

3

'BEING IN A CHAIR HAS NEVER STOPPED ME DOING ANYTHING I'VE EVER WANTED TO DO, AND SO MUCH OF IT IS ABOUT THE BELIEF YOU HAVE WITHIN YOURSELF.' — TANNI GREY-THOMPSON

# TANNI GREY-THOMPSON

## WHEELCHAIR RACER

Carys Davina 'Tanni' Grey-Thompson was born in Cardiff, UK in 1969. At birth she was diagnosed with spina bifida, causing her to lose mobility in her legs until she was completely paralysed at seven years old. Her parents never let her disability hold her back, and encouraged her to face the world head on. Tanni has spent her entire life fighting for herself and other people.

Tanni was always racing over kerbs and down streets in her wheelchair when she was young. She would watch the London Marathon on television and know that one day she would win that race – even though wheelchair racers weren't allowed to enter the London Marathon at the time. Thankfully, that rule was changed in 1983. In 1984, Tanni began competing in the Junior National Wheelchair Games, and by 17 she was a member of the British Wheelchair Racing squad.

In 1988, Tanni won her first Paralympic medal at the Seoul Paralympics, placing third in the 400 m race. Four years later, she won a gold medal at the 1992 London Wheelchair Marathon. That same year she won four gold medals and one silver at the 1992 Barcelona Paralympics. But it was just the beginning: Tanni also won gold medals during the 1996 Atlanta Paralympics, the 2000 Sydney Paralympics and the 2004 Athens Paralympics. In 2002, she became the first woman across the line at the London Wheelchair Marathon for a record-breaking sixth time.

In 1999, Tanni married paralympian Ian Thompson. It didn't distract her from racing for long – they honeymooned in Sempach, Switzerland, because it was an excellent training location. Tanni retired from racing in 2007. Today she fights to create a more inclusive world by working in the British parliament. In 2010 she became a peer in the House of Lords. Her main concerns are welfare reform, inclusivity in sports and securing equal rights for people with disabilities.

FIRST WOMAN TO BREAK THE 60-SECOND BARRIER DURING THE 400 M WHEELCHAIR RACE.

NICKNAMED 'TINY' BY HER SISTER, WHICH BECAME HER NAME TANNI.

HER PARENTS HAD TO FIGHT TO KEEP HER IN MAINSTREAM SCHOOL BECAUSE OF HER WHEELCHAIR.

SET 30 NEW WORLD RECORDS OVER THE COURSE OF HER CAREER.

ON THE BOARDS FOR TRANSPORT FOR LONDON, THE LONDON LEGACY DEVELOPMENT CORPORATION AND THE LONDON 2017 ORGANISING COMMITTEE.

# PAY AND MEDIA STATISTICS

Although women make up half the world's population, there is much less media coverage of women's professional sporting events than men's. Despite their breaking world records and playing intense and riveting games, sportswomen are not aired or promoted by TV networks nearly as much as men. This results in fewer resources and opportunities for female athletes.

## TELEVISION COVERAGE
### SPORTS COVERAGE ON CHANNELS
### KCBS, KNBC, AND KABC IN THE USA

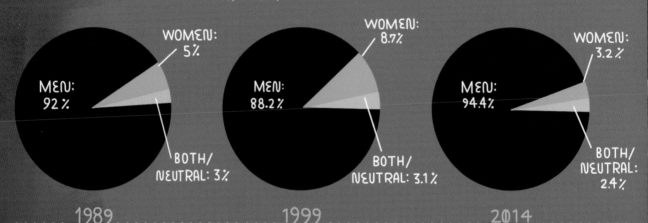

**1989**
- WOMEN: 5%
- MEN: 92%
- BOTH/NEUTRAL: 3%

**1999**
- WOMEN: 8.7%
- MEN: 88.2%
- BOTH/NEUTRAL: 3.1%

**2014**
- WOMEN: 3.2%
- MEN: 94.4%
- BOTH/NEUTRAL: 2.4%

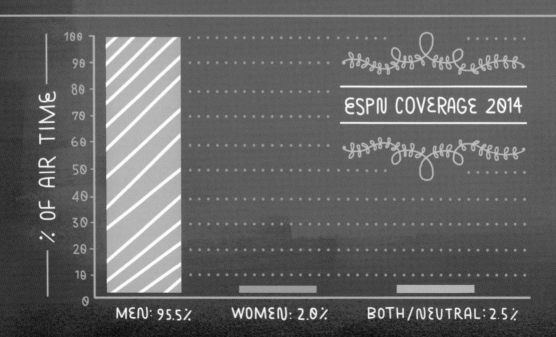

## ESPN COVERAGE 2014

% OF AIR TIME

MEN: 95.5%    WOMEN: 2.0%    BOTH/NEUTRAL: 2.5%

# PAY GAP

Globally, women are routinely paid less than men for the same work, and the world of professional sports is no exception. Here are a few examples of the pay gap in sport.

## GOLF

$320 MILLION IN TOTAL PRIZE MONEY

MEN'S 2014 PGA TOUR

$61.6 MILLION IN TOTAL PRIZE MONEY

WOMEN'S 2014 LPGA TOUR

## FOOTBALL

$9 MILLION FOR PLACING 11TH IN 2014 WORLD CUP

$2 MILLION FOR WINNING THE 2015 WORLD CUP

US MEN'S FOOTBALL TEAM

US WOMEN'S FOOTBALL TEAM

## BASKETBALL

### MEN'S
#### NBA IN THE 2015-16 SEASON

MIN SALARY $525,093

MAX SALARY $16.407 MILLION

### WOMEN'S
#### WNBA IN THE 2015 SEASON

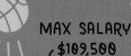

MAX SALARY $109,500

MIN SALARY $38,913

FIRST WOMAN FROM INDIA TO WIN A GOLD MEDAL AT THE ISSF WORLD CUP FINAL.

ONLY PERSON FROM INDIA TO WIN THE ISSF CHAMPIONS' TROPHY IN AIR RIFLE.

BECAME THE WORLD'S BEST AIR RIFLE SHOOTER IN THE 10 M EVENT IN 2002.

'SHOOTING IS A SPORT OF MENTAL POWER!' — ANJALI BHAGWAT

# ANJALI BHAGWAT

## MARKSWOMAN

Anjali Ramakanta Vedpathak-Bhagwat was born in 1969 in Mumbai, India. When it came time for Anjali to go to university, she didn't want to train for a normal desk job. Instead she joined the National Cadet Corps (NCC) at Kirti College so she could become one of the greatest rifle shooters in India.

Shooting was traditionally a man's sport, but with her incredible skill, Anjali would change her nation's perception of women in rifle shooting. At the NCC, shooting coach Sanjay Chakravarty noticed her talent and began to train her. Shooting requires immense physical and mental discipline. Anjali had strong muscles that allowed her to keep perfect posture while holding her 6-kg gun for hours at a time. Anjali learned to be aware of every variable on the range and to keep her attention focused on the balance of her weapon, the speed of the wind, and her own mental state so she could hit the target perfectly.

In 2002, Anjali made history at two international competitions: the Commonwealth Games and the International Shooting Sport Federation (ISSF) Championships. She had already won several gold medals at the 1999 and 2001 Commonwealth Shooting Championships, but she became the world's number one shooter at the 2002 Commonwealth Games. She took home five gold medals in the 10 m and 50 m (single and team) events. Anjali also became the first person from India to win the ISSF Champion of Champions combined-air-rifle event.

In 2003, Anjali scored a near-perfect 399/400 in the 10 m event, becoming the first Indian woman to win a gold medal at the ISSF World Cup. She was also awarded the Rajiv Gandhi Khel Ratna Award, India's highest sporting honour. She had cemented her legacy as one of the greatest rifle shooters in history.

Anjali continues to train, and has inspired more girls in India to take up shooting sports. India's women are now known as fierce competition on the shooting range.

WON MANY NATIONAL AWARDS, INCLUDING THE ARJUNA AWARD IN 2000.

NICKNAMED 'INDIAN SHOOTING QUEEN'.

IS TRAINED IN JUDO.

DOES YOGA TO KEEP HER MIND AND BODY FIT TO COMPETE.

SHE WAS FEATURED ON THE INDIAN TV SHOW MUJHE PANKH DE DO (WOMEN FOR CHANGE).

RAJIV GANDHI KHEL RATNA

REPRESENTED INDIA 3 TIMES AT THE OLYMPICS, IN THE 2000, 2004 AND 2008 GAMES.

WAS NAMED CHAMPION LADY RIDER IN 1990.

AWARDED A SPECIAL BAFTA FOR HER COVERAGE OF THE 2012 OLYMPICS.

WON THE SPECIAL ACHIEVEMENT AWARD AT THE WOMEN IN FILM AND TELEVISION AWARDS.

'WOMEN'S SPORT HELPS BREAK DOWN A LOT OF BARRIERS FOR WOMEN IN OTHER AREAS,
WHETHER IN RELIGION OR POLITICS.' — CLARE BALDING

# CLARE BALDING

## SPORTS BROADCASTER AND AMATEUR JOCKEY

Clare Balding was born in Hampshire, UK in 1971. Her family were no strangers to horse racing. Her father, uncle and grandmother were all accomplished jockeys and horse trainers, and Clare and her younger brother, Andrew, followed in the family tradition. Their first pony, Valkyrie, was a gift from the Queen, who owned horses trained by their father. Clare and Andrew practised falling off their horses on purpose so they would never be afraid of failing.

From 1988 to 1993, Clare was a leading amateur flat jockey, but in 1994 she began reporting horse races instead of riding in them. She would go on to become one of the UK's most renowned sports broadcasters.

In 1994, Clare started working with BBC National Radio as a trainee, and within a year she was on TV covering the highlights of Royal Ascot. By 1998 she was the lead presenter for all horse racing on the BBC. She then went on to become a leader in sports broadcasting for all different kinds of sports. During her career she has reported on six Olympic Games and four Paralympic Games for the BBC and other broadcasters. Along with presenting many other important sporting events such as Wimbledon, she also has her own show on BT Sport, called *The Clare Balding Show*, and a long-running radio programme called *Ramblings*.

Along with her success there have also been challenges. In 2009, Clare was diagnosed with cancer – but she fought back. She had her thyroid removed and was back covering the Epsom Derby that same year. Being in the public eye hasn't always been easy for Clare, either. The press has mocked her clothing for not being 'ladylike' and has made fun of her sexuality. But Clare always stands up for herself and others, and continues to do award-winning work. She has become a role model for girls everywhere and continues to be one of the most familiar faces of sports coverage on British television.

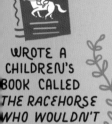

WROTE A CHILDREN'S BOOK CALLED *THE RACEHORSE WHO WOULDN'T GALLOP.*

NAMED SPORTS PRESENTER OF THE YEAR AND RACING JOURNALIST OF THE YEAR.

WROTE A MEMOIR CALLED *MY ANIMALS AND OTHER FAMILY.*

HAS HOSTED THE SHOWS *BRITAIN BY BIKE, BRITAIN'S HIDDEN HERITAGE, COUNTRYFILE* AND *BRITAIN'S BRIGHTEST.*

APPOINTED OFFICER OF THE MOST EXCELLENT ORDER OF THE BRITISH EMPIRE (OBE) IN 2013.

MOST DECORATED ARCHER IN KOREAN HISTORY.

EARNED 4 GOLD MEDALS IN THE OLYMPIC GAMES

THE INTERNATIONAL ARCHERY FEDERATION NAMED HER FEMALE ARCHER OF THE 20TH CENTURY.

'ARCHERY GIVES YOU CONVICTION. PEOPLE NEED CONVICTION ALL THE TIME: TO EAT WELL, TO DO ANYTHING. I WOULD SAY ARCHERY IS THE BEST SPORT FOR A GREAT LIFE.' — KIM SOO-NYUNG

# KIM SOO-NYUNG

## ARCHER

The 1988 Seoul Olympics marked an important time in South Korean history. That April, South Korea became a parliamentary democracy after years of military rule, and the country celebrated while hosting the Olympics. Each South Korean athlete's victory amplified the joy of their newfound freedom. None did so more than that of Kim Soo-Nyung, who delivered the most impressive archery performance the world had ever seen.

Kim Soo-Nyung was born in 1971 in South Korea. From the age of nine, archery was her passion. At 16, she set a new world record at a target distance of 30 m, and made the Olympic team. At the individual archery competition at the 1988 Olympics, the archers shot each round at a different distance from the target. At the 30-m distance, Kim Soo-Nyung shot all nine arrows in the target's centre 10-point area, earning a perfect score. She then completed the 50-m round and the 70-m round with an impressive total score of 344. With her teammates in the team event, Kim Soo-Nyung won her second Olympic gold medal, a tremendous victory for herself and for South Korea!

At the 1992 Olympics, Kim Soo-Nyung was expected to stomp to victory, but she lost the individual event to her friend and teammate Cho Youn-Jeong, and accepted her silver medal graciously. She then won her third gold medal, in the team event.

At 21, Kim Soo-Nyung was considered one of the greatest female archers ever. She decided to retire and focus on raising a family, but she couldn't resist the draw of the bow for long. In 1999, she made her comeback and qualified for the 2000 Olympics. Again she helped her team win a gold medal, and took home a bronze in the individual event. With a total of six Olympic medals, Kim Soo-Nyung is the most decorated archer in Korean history.

Kim Soo-Nyung's career set a new standard for female archers everywhere, and she will always be remembered as a part of the electrifying archery team at South Korea's historic 1988 Olympics.

THE SOUTH KOREAN WOMEN'S TEAM WON EVERY SINGLE ARCHERY MEDAL DURING THE 1988 OLYMPICS.

HER COACH CALLED HER 'THE VIPER'.

IN 2009, SHE WORKED AS A MEDIA DIRECTOR FOR THE WORLD ARCHERY CHAMPIONSHIPS.

WON GOLD MEDALS IN BOTH INDIVIDUAL AND TEAM EVENTS AT THE 1989 AND 1991 WORLD ARCHERY CHAMPIONSHIPS.

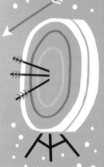

HELPED THE SOUTH KOREAN TEAM SET A NEW WORLD RECORD WITH 4,094 COMBINED POINTS AT THE 1992 OLYMPICS.

FOUNDER OF THE ALWAYS DREAM FOUNDATION.

WON BACK-TO-BACK WORLD SKATING CHAMPIONSHIPS.

FIRST ASIAN-AMERICAN WOMAN TO WIN AN OLYMPIC GOLD MEDAL.

'ALL THE ATHLETIC GLORY AND HONOURS ARE WONDERFUL. BUT SOMETIMES I COME FACE-TO-FACE WITH A DISADVANTAGED CHILD OR WITH A STRUGGLING MOTHER OR FATHER, AND I AM GRATEFUL FOR MY GIFTS AND I REDEDICATE MYSELF TO DOING WHATEVER I CAN TO HELP SOMEONE IN NEED.' – KRISTI YAMAGUCHI

# KRISTI YAMAGUCHI

## FIGURE-SKATER

Long before Kristi Yamaguchi represented America at the Olympics, her grandfather fought for America in the Second World War, but his family was confined in a Japanese-American internment camp, where Kristi's mother was born. Despite this injustice in her family history, Kristi would grow up to represent her country on the world stage and become the first Asian-American woman to win an Olympic gold medal.

Kristine Tsuya Yamaguchi was born in 1971 in California, USA. Like many little girls at the time, she watched Dorothy Hamill skate at the 1976 Olympics and wanted to be just like her. Kristi was born with club feet and had to wear corrective shoes and a brace when she was young. When Kristi asked to learn to ice-skate, her mum thought it would be a great way to strengthen her legs. After countless lessons and years of practising, Kristi started competing nationally.

In the 1985 US Championship, she skated with Rudy Galindo, with whom she won national titles in 1986, 1989 and 1990. After Kristi and Rudi finished fifth at the 1989 and 1990 World Championships, Kristi focused on singles skating. It was a good move — she won gold at the 1991 World Championship with a perfect 6.0 score for artistic composition. After years of coming second at Nationals, she finally won a gold medal in 1992.

She would compete in her first Olympics that same year. Kristi wowed the Olympic crowd and the judges, and the gold medal was hers. Newspapers described her performance as so beautiful it was like 'the melodies were written on her skates'. That year she would also win the 1992 World Championship for the second time, becoming the first American to complete the 'Triple Crown' of skating since Dorothy Hamill in 1976.

Kristi's success gave her a platform to do good in the world. Through her Always Dream Foundation she promotes childhood literacy and helps disadvantaged students follow their dreams.

HER 1992 OLYMPIC PERFORMANCE WAS TO 'MALAGUEÑA'.

GOOD LUCK!

DOROTHY HAMILL WISHED HER GOOD LUCK BEFORE KRISTI PERFORMED AT THE 1992 OLYMPICS!

IN THE US FIGURE-SKATING HALL OF FAME AND THE WORLD FIGURE-SKATING HALL OF FAME.

THE 'TRIPLE CROWN' OF SKATING IS WINNING THE NATIONAL CHAMPIONSHIP, WORLD CHAMPIONSHIP AND OLYMPICS IN THE SAME YEAR.

HER DOROTHY HAMILL DOLL WAS HER FAVOURITE TOY!

STARS

APPEARED ON THE TV SHOW *STARS ON ICE.*

HAS WON THE WOMEN'S ASP WORLD CHAMPIONSHIP 7 TIMES.

FOUNDER OF THE AIM FOR THE STARS FOUNDATION.

INDUCTED INTO THE SURFING AUSTRALIA HALL OF FAME IN 2006.

'I WILL GO AFTER WHAT I WANT WITH RECKLESS ABANDON UNTIL I HAVE IT, IF IT MEANS THAT MUCH TO ME.' – LAYNE BEACHLEY

# LAYNE BEACHLEY

## SURFER

Layne Collette Beachley was born in Australia in 1972. Her mother died when she was six, and when she was eight she found out she had been adopted. Layne thinks this sparked her motivation to become the world's very best at something. That something would be surfing, and she would become the longest-reigning world surfing champion in history.

As a teenager, Layne hung around surfing pros and learned everything she could from them. It worked — by age 16 she was a professional surfer and competed in the Association of Surfing Professionals (ASP) Women's World Tour. She was hard on herself, always pushing to be the very best. The ocean can be dangerous, and Layne would often ignore injuries to keep competing. In 1993, she won her first pro surfing competition. That same year she was also diagnosed with chronic fatigue syndrome. Layne battled depression throughout her career too, but by getting help, being self-aware and taking care of herself, she overcame the dark moments so she could enjoy her passions: surfing and winning.

Layne surfed all over the world, and the 1998 Women's ASP World Championship was the start of her legendary winning streak. She won the World Championship six years in a row from 1998 to 2003. No man or woman has ever won so many consecutive world surfing competitions. In 2003 and 2004, she was named *Surfer* magazine Female Surfer of the Year. The awards and accolades kept piling up, and in 2006 she won her seventh World Championship, becoming the winningest woman in surf history.

In 2008, she retired from surfing. As a chairperson of Surfing Australia, she is one of the only female world champions to have this kind of influence over her sport. She now helps ensure funding for women's surf tournaments and fights for equal pay for female pro surfers. She started the foundation Aim for the Stars, which awards scholarships and support to girls in art, business, science and sport. She wants to help all girls dream big and achieve their goals.

HAS HAD 29 WORLD TOUR VICTORIES.

WORKED 4 DIFFERENT JOBS TO SUPPORT HERSELF WHILE SURFING PROFESSIONALLY IN 1995.

WORKED FOR 15 YEARS ON THE ASSOCIATION OF SURFING PROFESSIONALS BOARD.

TRAVELS THE WORLD GIVING MOTIVATIONAL SPEECHES.

AWARDED AN OFFICER OF THE ORDER OF AUSTRALIA.

HER LUMBAR SPINE WAS CRUSHED IN A FALL DURING THE WORLD CHAMPIONSHIPS, BUT SHE STILL CAME IN FIRST.

2001 AND 2002 FIFA WORLD PLAYER OF THE YEAR.

IN THE US NATIONAL SOCCER HALL OF FAME
AND THE WORLD FOOTBALL HALL OF FAME.

WON OLYMPIC GOLD MEDALS IN 1996 AND 2004
AND A SILVER MEDAL IN 2000 WITH TEAM USA.

'TAKE YOUR VICTORIES, WHATEVER THEY MAY BE, CHERISH THEM, USE THEM, BUT DON'T SETTLE FOR THEM.' – MIA HAMM

# MIA HAMM

## FOOTBALL PLAYER

Mariel Margaret 'Mia' Hamm was born in 1972 in Alabama, USA. At 15, Mia became the youngest person ever on the US national women's team. At 17, she attended the University of North Carolina, where she won the 1989, 1990, 1992 and 1993 NCAA Championships with her team. Mia paused her studies to compete with the US team, and won the 1991 Women's World Cup.

In 1996, Mia was ready to compete in the Olympics with Team USA. That year, Mia's brother Garrett, who'd lived with aplastic anaemia since the age of 16, received a fatal diagnosis. Despite his illness, he came to watch Mia's Olympic victory. Sadly, he passed away in 1997. In her brother's honour, Mia created the Mia Hamm Foundation, which raises money for girls' sport and for people who need bone marrow transplants.

Mia continued to push the boundaries in women's football. In 1999, she scored her 108th international goal, setting a new world record for men's and women's football. But victory on the field did not mean equality. FIFA, football's governing body, wanted the 1999 Women's World Cup to play smaller venues, afraid no one wanted to watch it. Marla Messing, head of their organising committee, demanded that FIFA showcase the women's teams in large stadiums, just like they did for the men. For each women's game, the stadium was packed with fans.

In the final game of the tournament, over 90,000 spectators packed into the Rose Bowl stadium in California to watch the United States play China. After 30 minutes of overtime, it came down to penalty kicks. Mia was nervous; penalty shots weren't her strong suit. But she focused on the ball and scored! Her teammate Brandi Chastain scored the next shot, and the US women won, changing the way Americans saw women's football and paving the way for countless girls to get out and play.

In 2001, Mia Hamm helped start the first US football league for women, the Women's United Soccer Association. Today Mia continues to fight for equality in women's sport.

MIA AND HER FAMILY WERE INTRODUCED TO FOOTBALL WHEN HER DAD WAS STATIONED IN ITALY.

WON 3 ESPY AWARDS.

SET A RECORD IN 2004 OF 58 INTERNATIONAL GOALS, A FIRST FOR MALE AND FEMALE FOOTBALL PLAYERS.

NAMED SOCCER USA'S FEMALE ATHLETE OF THE YEAR FROM 1994 TO 1998.

BORN WITH A PARTIALLY CLUBBED FOOT.

HAS A DEGREE IN POLITICAL SCIENCE.

4-TIME OLYMPIC GOLD MEDALLIST

3-TIME WNBA MVP.

IN THE NAISMITH MEMORIAL BASKETBALL HALL OF FAME.

'IT IS NOT OUR FAULT WE WERE BORN GIRLS. WE JUST WANT TO PLAY TOO. WE JUST WANT TO HAVE OUR EQUAL SPACE AND PLACE.' – LISA LESLIE

# LISA LESLIE

## BASKETBALL PLAYER

Lisa Deshaun Leslie was born in 1972 and raised by a single mum in California, USA. Lisa's mum showed her that you can be strong and feminine at the same time, even while she did tough jobs such as driving an 18-wheeler truck and welding.

Lisa started playing basketball in middle school. She was not only tall (six foot at the age of 12), she was a natural at the sport, making the papers when she scored 101 points in the first half of one game. Lisa set two life goals: to get a sport scholarship to university and to play in the Olympics.

Lisa was the star player on her high school basketball team. In 1990, she entered the University of Southern California on a full scholarship. Opportunities for women and men in university basketball were different. The men were being scouted by the NBA, but the WNBA did not yet exist. Lisa put her education first and worked towards her dream of representing the United States in the Olympics.

In 1996, she qualified for the US Olympic basketball team and won an Olympic gold medal. That same year, the WNBA was created. In 1997, at the first WNBA games, Lisa played centre for the Los Angeles Sparks. By 2001, nearly 2.5 million fans attended the WNBA games. In 2002, Lisa made history as the first woman ever to dunk during a professional game, and the crowd went wild.

In her 12 years playing for the Sparks, Lisa won three MVP awards, helped her team win two championships and scored over 6,200 points. With the US Olympic team, she earned gold medals at the 2000, 2004 and 2008 Games, becoming one of the most decorated basketball players in Olympic history.

In 2009, Lisa retired. She wanted to show the world that she was a powerful woman on and off the court. She earned a MBA, and became an owner of the Sparks. Lisa is one of the greatest basketball players ever and a role model to girls everywhere.

FIRST PLAYER IN THE WNBA TO SCORE OVER 6,000 CAREER POINTS.

HER BOOK IS TITLED DON'T LET THE LIPSTICK FOOL YOU.

NAMED 1994 NATIONAL PLAYER OF THE YEAR IN HER FINAL YEAR OF UNIVERSITY.

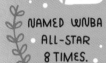

NAMED WNBA ALL-STAR 8 TIMES.

ALWAYS WORE LIPSTICK AND DID HER HAIR BEFORE A GAME TO SHOW THE WORLD YOU CAN BE FEMININE AND STRONG.

SHE IS 6'5.

WON GOLD AT THE 1992 AND 1994 IIHF WOMEN'S WORLD CHAMPIONSHIPS

WON A SILVER MEDAL IN THE 1998 OLYMPIC HOCKEY TOURNAMENT.

FIRST WOMAN TO PLAY FOR THE NATIONAL HOCKEY LEAGUE.

'I'VE HAD PEOPLE COME UP TO ME AND SAY "MY DAUGHTER WANTS TO BE LIKE YOU. YOU'RE SUCH AN INSPIRATION"...THAT PROBABLY THE MOST SATISFYING THING I DID, TO KNOW THAT MY STORY HELPED OTHER PEOPLE.' – MANON RHÉAUME

# MANON RHÉAUME

## ICE HOCKEY GOALKEEPER

**PARTICIPATED IN NHL CHARITY GAMES.**

**WROTE AN AUTOBIOGRAPHY, ALONE IN FRONT OF THE NET.**

**HER DAD HELPED HER BUILD HER PROTECTIVE GEAR AND PADDING.**

Manon Rhéaume was the first woman ever to play in the National Hockey League (NHL). Ice hockey pucks whizzed toward her at over 160 km an hour. She was an expert in blocking those goals and had the bruises to prove it. Manon was born in 1972 in Québec, Canada. Like many Canadian children, Manon started playing ice hockey when she was little. Her father would flood their garden to create

a homemade skating rink, and six-year-old Manon would be goalie for her brother's team. A natural, before long she was playing on the boys' team at school.

After high school, Manon became the first woman to play on a men's Junior A hockey team, the minor league in ice hockey. She was a great, tough goalie. Once during a game, a puck hit her right in the face, shattering her protective mask and leaving her with a bloody gash above her eye. She never left the ice, defending the goal until the whistle blew and she could get stitched up.

At the age of 20, Manon joined a training camp for a new NHL team, the Tampa Bay Lightning. Many of the coaches thought she was only there for publicity. Manon didn't care. She was ready to prove herself, and the male players didn't go easy on her. Some would slap pucks at her as hard as possible, embarrassed at not being able to score against a female goalie. Manon played well and earned a place on the team. In 1992, she became the first woman to play in the NHL.

Manon also played goalie for Canada in the World Women's Hockey Championship. In 1992 and 1994, she helped her team win gold. She continued to play for various pro ice hockey teams, including the Atlanta Knights, the Tallahassee Tiger Sharks and the Reno Renegades. In 1998, she won an Olympic silver medal.

In 2008, Manon set up the Manon Rhéaume Foundation to help girls fulfil their aspirations. By watching her tough it out, girls everywhere have been inspired to start playing ice hockey.

**ALSO PLAYED PROFESSIONAL ROLLER HOCKEY.**

**HER TWO SONS ALSO LOVE PLAYING ICE HOCKEY.**

**HER FIRST MAJOR JUNIOR TEAM WAS THE TROIS-RIVIERES DRAVEURS.**

CONSIDERED ONE OF THE GREATEST PLAYERS IN TABLE TENNIS HISTORY.

WON 4 OLYMPIC GOLD MEDALS.

VOTED CHINESE FEMALE ATHLETE OF THE CENTURY.

'STRENGTH IS THE KEY TO SUCCESS. AFTER YEARS OF PLAYING, STUDYING AND WORKING, I'VE REALISED I CAN ONLY PROVE MYSELF AND WIN RESPECT FROM OTHERS WITH MY STRENGTH.' – DENG YAPING

# DENG YAPING

## TABLE TENNIS PLAYER

4'11"

Deng Yaping was born in 1973 in the Henan province of China. She started playing table tennis aged five. It didn't take long for her to start winning provincial junior championships, and by age 13, she had won the national championship. Despite her skills, the sporting community did not take her seriously because of her size — she was four foot eleven — and she was even arbitrarily disqualified from China's national team because of this. But, with her lightning-fast speed and agility, she just kept winning table tennis games until they could no longer deny her a place on the national team. She went on to become the world doubles champion in 1989 and the world singles champion in 1991.

At the 1992 Olympics, Deng won gold medals in doubles and singles. The singles match was a nail-biter between Deng and her own doubles partner, Qiao Hong, with Deng winning 23-21.

In 1995 and 1997, Deng became the world singles and doubles champion again. In 1996, she earned two more Olympic gold medals, one in doubles and another in singles. No other table tennis player in history, male or female, has won this many world titles. She has always said that strength was the key to her success.

Deng retired in 1997 aged 24. That year she was elected to the International Olympic Committee Athletes Commission; she later helped to organise the 2008 Olympics in Beijing. Since she was no longer competing, education became her priority. She earned an undergraduate degree from Tsinghua University, a master's degree from the University of Nottingham and a PhD from the University of Cambridge.

Deng Yaping proved that no matter your size, you can have great strength and skill. She showed China and the world that talent and determination are what's needed to become a champion.

RANKED THE WORLD'S #1 TABLE TENNIS PLAYER FOR 8 YEARS.

HAS PLAYED TABLE TENNIS USING A WOODEN SPOON INSTEAD OF A PADDLE AS A GIMMICK.

WAS A TORCHBEARER AT THE 2008 LIGHTING CEREMONY OF THE OLYMPIC FLAME.

HAS WON 18 WORLD CHAMPION TITLES.

THE 1992 OLYMPIC SINGLES FINAL WAS A HEATED MATCH AGAINST HER DOUBLES PARTNER. DENG YAPING WON 23-21.

HER DOUBLES PARTNERS HAVE INCLUDED HONG QIAO AND YING YANG.

MEMBER OF THE ITALIAN PARLIAMENT.

HAS WON 16 WORLD CHAMPIONSHIP GOLD MEDALS.

6-TIME OLYMPIC GOLD MEDALLIST IN FOIL.

'MY FOIL HAS BEEN WITH ME SINCE I WAS LITTLE MORE THAN 6 YEARS OLD, AND TOGETHER WE'VE SHARED
EMOTIONS, DISAPPOINTMENTS, MEDALS, MISFORTUNES AND TEARS OF BOTH JOY AND ANGER.' - VALENTINA VEZZALI

# VALENTINA VEZZALI

## FENCER

Maria Valentina Vezzali was born in 1974 in Jesi, Italy. When she was six, she started training at a local fencing school. There are three types of fencing weapon: foil, épée, and sabre. Valentina fenced foil, meaning she could score points only by striking with the tip of her blade on her opponent's torso. By the age of 10, she had won her first national title in the junior division.

Valentina would never settle for just winning — she wanted to be the very best. After each victory, she would immediately set a new goal for herself, a new challenge to conquer. In 1996, she made her Olympic debut and won two medals, a gold in the team event and a silver in the individual. All of this would satisfy some, but not Valentina. She set her goals even higher and worked to become one of the world's greatest fencers.

In 1999, Valentina won her first individual title at the World Fencing Championships. The next year, she fulfilled her dream of winning gold in both the individual and the team events at the 2000 Olympics. At the 2004 Olympics, she again won gold in the individual foil event. The 2008 Olympics was her first as a mother, and by winning an individual gold medal and a team bronze in the team event, she showed the world that motherhood and sporting competition are not mutually exclusive.

Valentina wanted to be the best, and her medal haul is legendary. She is the only fencer to win individual gold medals in three consecutive Olympics. In the 2012 London Olympics, Valentina won another bronze and a gold, making her the most decorated female fencer in history.

Throughout her career, Valentina has been active in many charities including the 'Run for Food' campaign and the '1billionhungry' project to end world hunger. In 2013, she was elected to the Italian Parliament's Chamber of Deputies. She retired from fencing in 2016 as a legend in the sport.

FENCING BEGAN IN THE 19TH CENTURY AS A WAY TO PRACTISE DUELLING.

I RESPECT MY OPPONENTS!

THINKS ALL POLITICIANS SHOULD HAVE MORE SPORTSMANSHIP.

WAS TAUGHT FENCING BY ENZO TRICOLLI, WHO LEARNED THE SPORT IN A POW CAMP IN WWII.

SOMETIMES SANG TO HERSELF OR PRAYED TO HER DAD BEFORE SHE COMPETED.

YUNGA
YOUTH & UNITED NATIONS GLOBAL ALLIANCE

BECAME A YUNGA AMBASSADOR IN 2009.

HAS WON 6 GOLD WORLD CHAMPIONSHIP MEDALS IN ROWING.

THE MOST DECORATED FEMALE ATHLETE IN BRITAIN.

FIRST FEMALE ROWER TO WIN MEDALS IN 4 CONSECUTIVE OLYMPICS.

'SPORT TEACHES YOU SO MUCH; HOW TO MANAGE SUCCESS AND NEGOTIATE FAILURE, HOW TO BE PART OF A TEAM, HOW TO BE THE BEST LEADER YOU CAN BE — AND HOW TO MAKE YOUR DREAMS COME TRUE.' —KATHERINE GRAINGER

# KATHERINE GRAINGER

## ROWER

Katherine Grainger was born in 1975 in Glasgow, UK. There is nothing this woman can't do. She is the Chancellor of Oxford Brookes University, has a PhD in criminal law and is the most decorated female athlete in Britain. With brains and brawl, Katherine has given it her all on the water. She has become a world-famous rower and a role model for girls everywhere.

Katherine began rowing in 1993 while attending the University of Edinburgh. Within three years she was named her university's most outstanding athlete and was awarded the Eva Bailey Trophy twice. In 1997, she won her first international rowing competition at the Under-23 Rowing Championships. It would not be long before she was winning medals at the Olympics.

Rowing events at the Olympics can be done alone (singles) or together in teams of two, four or eight. Katherine won her first Olympic silver medal in the quadruple scull event during the 2000 Sydney Olympics, and it was the first time Olympic medals were awarded to women in the history of rowing. She went on to win silver medals at the 2004 Athens Olympics in the coxless pairs and the 2008 Olympics in the quadruple sculls event. But her real goal was an Olympic gold medal.

During the 2012 London games, she finally finished first with rowing partner Anna Watkins in the double sculls event. The gold medal was hers and her dream had come true! Katherine became the first female rower to win medals in four consecutive Olympic Games. She made it five at the 2016 Olympics in Rio, when she won a silver after returning to rowing following a two-year break.

In 2017 Katherine was named Dame Katherine Grainger to honour her excellence in sport, and became chair of UK Sport, which aims to lead Britain to world-class success.

BECAME FIRST WOMAN TO WIN SCOTLAND'S SPORTSPERSON OF THE YEAR IN 2009.

DREAMS DO COME TRUE

WROTE HER AUTOBIOGRAPHY DREAMS DO COME TRUE.

PRESENTED THE ROWING WORLD CUP ON THE BBC.

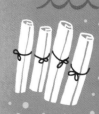

HAS BEEN AWARDED HONORARY DOCTORATES FROM 7 PRESTIGIOUS UNIVERSITIES.

IS A FELLOW OF KING'S COLLEGE LONDON AND REGENT OF EDINBURGH UNIVERSITY.

BROKE THE WORLD RECORD FOR FASTEST SOLO SAIL.

PROMOTES SUSTAINABILITY AND THE IDEA OF A CIRCULAR ECONOMY THROUGH HER FOUNDATION.

SHE BECAME THE YOUNGEST PERSON TO BE NAMED DAME COMMANDER OF THE BRITISH EMPIRE.

'THIS WORLD, THAT I THOUGHT AS A CHILD WAS THE BIGGEST, MOST ADVENTUROUS PLACE YOU

# ELLEN MACARTHUR

## LONG-DISTANCE YACHTSWOMAN

Ellen Patricia MacArthur was born in Britain in 1976. She first went on a yacht at the age of four. By eight, she'd begun saving up for a boat of her own. Ellen's parents always gave her the freedom and support to go out and seek adventure, even when she decided to sail the world's most dangerous seas. By 18, Ellen had earned her yachtmaster qualification; that year she sailed solo around Great Britain. In 1996 she participated in a race across the Atlantic from Canada to France, and came third. It was a great achievement, but Ellen wanted to become the fastest sailor of all time.

THE BOAT ELLEN SAILED AROUND THE WORLD.

23 METRES TALL

MULTIHULL

Ellen's goal was to make a non-stop sailing trip around the world and to break the world record for this feat, set by Francis Joyon: 72 days, 22 hours, 54 minutes and 22 seconds. Sailing solo can be incredibly dangerous, but Ellen was not afraid to test her limits. In 2004, she set sail from England and started breaking records: speed to the equator, to the Cape of Good Hope and to Australia's Cape Leeuwin. It was not all smooth sailing: she severely burned her arm while switching out generators and began lagging behind the record time by four days after crossing the equator. But with hard work and determination Ellen broke the world record for sailing around the world, with a time of 71 days, 14 hours, 18 minutes and 33 seconds. Ellen was the fastest person on the seas!

Ellen retired from sailing in 2009, turning her focus to charity. In 2010, she founded the Ellen MacArthur Foundation, which promotes a 'circular economy', in which we reuse and recycle instead of making new products that end up as rubbish. She was inspired by how she used resources at sea, where survival depended on using — and reusing — only essentials. Her record for the fastest solo sail around the world has been broken, but she broke barriers and now works for a more sustainable future.

# INFLUENTIAL SPORTS TEAMS

As a team, athletes can reach large crowds and new heights. Here are a few of the amazing women's sports teams that have changed history.

## BLOOMER GIRLS, 1866

As early as 1866, US women played baseball on teams called Bloomer Girls. They became popular in the 1890s. The teams were mixed and usually had only one or two male players. They would travel the country challenging different towns' male baseball teams. These teams led to the creation of the first professional All-American Girls Softball League in 1943 and the many modern women's teams of today.

## TENNESSEE STATE UNIVERSITY TIGERBELLES, 1950s AND 60s

With hardly any funding, the Tigerbelles athletics team included some of the greatest sprinters in history. During the 1950s, 60s and early 70s, Tennessee State University was the training ground for several US athletics stars. The teams consisted of some of the most influential people in athletics, including Chandra Cheeseborough, Wilma Rudolph and Wyomia Tyus. Their coach, Edward Temple, was hugely influential in fostering and shaping their talent. Forty Tigerbelles runners went on to become Olympians. The Tigerbelles were underdogs but proved to the world what women are capable of.

## US NATIONAL SOCCER TEAM, 2015

The 2015 United States versus Japan FIFA Women's World Cup Final was the most-watched football game of all time in the United States. The US women's victory showed the world the skill and strength of American women. Game viewership — over 23 million — surpassed even the legendary 1999 Women's World Cup Final.

The women of the US national football team have made strides toward pay equality. The team was ranked number one in the world, projected to bring in over $17 million in revenue in 2017. However, they were still being paid thousands of dollars less than the US men's team, which was losing money. The women of the US team went public with this pay gap, and in 2016, the US Senate took their side and unanimously voted in favour of a resolution to 'eliminate gender pay inequity and treat all athletes with the same respect and dignity'. Although this resolution is not law, it is a step in the right direction to pressure FIFA to comply with the Equal Pay Act.

## THE WOMEN OF THE REFUGEE OLYMPIC TEAM, 2016

In 2016, the Olympics included the first-ever refugee team. The 10 people (four women) on the team had all fled their home countries because they were at risk of death. With no citizenship, these athletes competed under the Olympic flag.

The team included Anjelina Lohalith and Rose Lokonyen, who both escaped the violent war in South Sudan and competed as runners during the Games. Yolande Mabika, a judoka, was also on the team. As a child, Yolande was separated from her parents during the war in the Democratic Republic of the Congo. She then had to escape an abusive judo coach and is now a refugee living in Brazil. The final woman on the team was swimmer Yusra Mardini. With her family, she fled the bombings and terrorist attacks in Syria. When their escape boat's motor stopped working in the middle of the Mediterranean Sea, Yusra, her sister and two other people got into the cold water and pushed the boat for hours until they reached the safety of Greece.

These courageous athletes showed the world how strong they are and gained a platform to bring awareness to the plight of refugees around the world.

HAS WON 3 ITU PARATRIATHLON WORLD CHAMPIONSHIPS.

WON A BRONZE MEDAL AT THE 2016 PARALYMPICS.

IS A US ARMY VETERAN AND WAS AWARDED A BRONZE STAR AND THE PURPLE HEART IN 2005.

'WE HAVE THE POWER TO CHOOSE OUR STORY ... I WANT TO BE KNOWN AS SOMEONE WHO TURNED SOMETHING VERY TRAGIC INTO TRIUMPH.' – MELISSA STOCKWELL

# MELISSA STOCKWELL

## PARATRIATHLETE

Melissa Stockwell bravely served as a US Army lieutenant in the Iraq War. Aged 24, she was caught in a roadside bomb explosion in Baghdad. To save her life, doctors amputated one of her legs.

Melissa was born in Michigan, USA in 1980. Before she served her country in the military, she dreamed of representing the United States as an Olympic athlete. In 2005, she retired from the Army. With just one leg, Melissa needed to re-learn how to walk with a prosthetic and to figure out what she would do with her life. She eventually re-learned to walk, run, swim and ride a bike. She even learned to ski. After skiing down a mountain, Melissa realised that she could still become a champion athlete.

During rehab, she was introduced to the Paralympics. Her dream of being an Olympian could still come true — as a Paralympian! She enjoyed her rehab swimming sessions and thought she could improve her speed enough to make the Paralympic team. With the help of coach Jimi Flowers at the US Olympic Training Center, she made the Paralympic swimming team and competed at the 2008 Beijing Paralympics.

After that, Melissa was invited to compete in the paratriathlon. Triathlons are tricky — as well as working on her stamina, she had to practise taking off her running prosthetic leg to swim, then quickly putting on her biking leg, all within her competition time. In 2009, she completed her first triathlon of the same distance as the Olympic triathlon. She won the 2010 International Triathlon Union (ITU) World Championships and won the gold again in 2011 and 2012. In 2016, at the very first Paralympic triathlon event, she won a bronze medal – and fulfilled her dream of standing on the Olympic podium.

Melissa Stockwell turned the greatest obstacle of her life into an opportunity. She works hard to give other athletes with disabilities new opportunities.

**NAMED FEMALE PARATRIATHLETE OF THE YEAR IN 2010 AND 2011 BY USA TRIATHLON.**

**RAN WITH AN AMERICAN FLAG DURING THE 2008 OLYMPIC CLOSING CEREMONIES.**

**HAS WORKED AS A PROSTHETIST.**

**WON THE MILDRED 'BABE' DIDRIKSON ZAHARIAS COURAGE AWARD IN 2014.**

**INVOLVED IN THE WOUNDED WARRIOR PROJECT AND THE CHALLENGED ATHLETES FOUNDATION TO HELP RECENT AMPUTEES.**

**GAVE BIRTH TO HER SON IN 2014.**

# SERENA WILLIAMS

## TENNIS PLAYER

SISTERS AND BFFS!

LIVED WITH HER SISTER VENUS FOR OVER 30 YEARS AND LOVED IT!

LOVES KARAOKE.

THE SERENA WILLIAMS FUND HAS WORKED TO CREATE EQUAL ACCESS TO EDUCATION AROUND THE WORLD.

Serena Jameka Williams was born in 1981 in Michigan, USA. The family moved to Compton, California, where she and her older sister Venus learned to play tennis. Their father dreamed of his daughters becoming the world's greatest tennis players, and started training the sisters on a public court when they were four and five. He would train them throughout their careers. At first, Venus was the prodigy and the star — Serena did not yet have the powerful stroke she is known for today. Serena adored Venus and wanted to be just like her sister.

At age 14, Serena played her first professional event. Venus was already a tennis superstar, but Serena soon caught up with her, and in 1999, she won her first US Open singles title. At the 2000 Olympics, the two teamed up to win a doubles gold medal. They also won all of the Grand Slam doubles titles from 1999 to 2001; these plus their Olympic gold made a Career Golden Slam. The Williams sisters became international superstars.

By 2003, Serena was world number one. She won the four Grand Slam titles - the French Open, Wimbledon, US Open and Australian Open — in a row, a feat which is now affectionately named the 'Serena Slam'. She continued to dominate in singles and also teamed up with Venus to win multiple Grand Slam and major tournament doubles titles.

In 2010, a series of injuries kept her off the court. She would have to build herself back up from the bottom. By 2011 she was making one of the greatest comebacks in sporting history. Her Olympic gold medals in 2012 in both singles and doubles led to her second Career Golden Slam. By 2013, she was once again the number one player in the world. In 2017, she broke another taboo and showed how amazingly strong women's bodies can be, winning the Australian Open while eight weeks pregnant.

Serena has won 23 Grand Slam singles titles to date. She is a gladiator, role model, fashion icon and philanthropist who has inspired the world.

2015 SPORTS ILLUSTRATED SPORTSPERSON OF THE YEAR.

HAS APPEARED IN COUNTLESS TV SHOWS AND MOVIES AND ON MAGAZINE COVERS.

THEIR MUM STYLED THE WILLIAMS SISTERS WITH THEIR SIGNATURE BEADED BRAIDS FOR THEIR TENNIS DEBUT.

FIRST AND ONLY WOMAN TO WIN AN INDYCAR RACE

FIRST WOMAN TO LEAD LAPS DURING THE INDIANAPOLIS 500.

HOLDS THE RECORD IN THE INDY RACING LEAGUE FOR THE MOST CONSECUTIVE FINISHED RACES.

'DON'T TRY AND BE LIKE SOMEONE ELSE 'CAUSE YOU NEVER CAN BE. YOU HAVE YOUR OWN PATH AND THAT'S WHAT MAKES YOU UNIQUE AND THAT'S WHAT MAKES YOU INTERESTING.' – DANICA PATRICK

# DANICA PATRICK

## RACECAR DRIVER

IN 2004, SHE BECAME THE FIRST WOMAN TO PLACE ON THE PODIUM AT THE TOYOTA ATLANTIC SERIES.

IN 2013, WAS THE FIRST WOMAN TO WIN THE POLE POSITION IN A SPRINT CUP SERIES.

YOGA IS PART OF HER WORKOUT ROUTINE.

Open-wheel racecar driving is one of the world's most dangerous sports. Imagine going over 320 kph, where a moment's distraction could mean a fatal crash. With each turn, the amount of G-force pressure on a racer's body makes it almost impossible to breathe. Drivers build their upper body strength to steer the car against this force; they must engage every muscle to stay seated, feet on the pedals and hands on the wheel.

Danica Sue Patrick was born in 1982 and grew up in Illinois, USA. At the age of 10, Danica started go-kart racing and immediately crashed straight into a wall. Shaken but not deterred, she was ready to try again! In 1994, 1996 and 1997, she won the World Karting Association Grand National Championship. At 16, she was offered a sponsorship to train

in Europe and to compete in the British National Series. In 2000, she became the most successful American ever in Britain's Formula Ford Festival race, coming second.

In 2005, Danica competed at the famous Indianapolis 500 race. She was only the fourth woman ever to compete there, and led for 19 laps, a historic first for a woman. She finished fourth and continued to perform well in IndyCar races. She was featured on the cover of *Sports Illustrated* and won the Rookie of the Year Award, but it was not enough. She wanted to win the race! In 2008, in the Indy Japan 300, Danica led in her final lap. Over five seconds ahead of the car behind her, she crossed the finish line. The chequered flag went up, and Danica became the first woman in history to win an IndyCar race!

In 2010, Danica entered the world of NASCAR, making her one of the most famous sports stars in the USA. Danica continues to lead laps, break records and show the world that racing is for girls too.

FIRST WOMAN TO LEAD A NASCAR RACE UNDER GREEN FLAG CONDITIONS.

HAS BEEN IN 13 SUPER BOWL ADS.

WAS NAMED INDY RACING LEAGUE'S MOST POPULAR DRIVER FROM 2005 TO 2007.

FIRST FEMALE BOXING CHAMPION IN BOTH THE OLYMPIC GAMES AND THE COMMONWEALTH GAMES.

FIRST WOMAN TO WIN AN OLYMPIC MEDAL IN BOXING.

IS A MEMBER OF THE ORDER OF THE BRITISH EMPIRE.

'PEOPLE [NOW] DON'T REALLY SEE MALE OR FEMALE. NOW WHEN THEY SEE ME BOX, THEY JUST SEE A GOOD BOXER.' —NICOLA ADAMS

# NICOLA ADAMS

## BOXER

Nicola Adams was born in 1982 and grew up in Leeds, UK. For 116 years, women's boxing was seen as 'wrong', 'unladylike' and 'dangerous'. In 1996, the ban on women's boxing was finally lifted, and the Amateur Boxing Association of England slowly opened its doors to everyone. Luckily for the boxing world, that year Nicola Adams discovered the sport and determined to become the greatest boxer at the Olympics! Olympic boxing was not even open to women at the time, and Nicola was the only girl in her boxing programme. But she knew that with hard work, she could one day accomplish her dream.

Becoming a world champion boxer would not be easy, physically or financially. Her mum, always supportive, often worked until midnight to pay the bills. Nicola also worked to help with the cost of competing and travel. In 2007, she became the first British woman awarded a medal in a major boxing tournament, coming second at the European Championship. The next year she won a silver medal at the World Championships.

In 2009, Nicola fell down the stairs while on the way to an important match. With a fresh fracture in her spine, she still won the fight. The injury put her on bed rest for three months and threatened to end her career, but she was back in the ring a year later, winning another World Championships silver medal. She won silver again at this competition in 2012. In 2011, she won the European Union Championships and qualified to compete at the 2012 Olympic Games in the first-ever female boxing event.

The 2012 Olympics was the first time that many spectators saw women's boxing. The fight between Nicola and China's Ran Cancan was intense, each hitting hard and at lightning speed. Nicola's powerful punches connected, and she became the first woman in boxing history to win an Olympic gold medal!

Nicola has influenced many girls to start boxing. In 2016, she took the World Championship title and another gold medal at the Rio Olympics, realising her lifelong dream for a second time.

WON THE 2015 BOXING TITLE AT THE EUROPEAN GAMES.

HAS ACTED AS AN EXTRA IN A FEW BRITISH SOAP OPERAS.

IS AN AMBASSADOR FOR THE FIGHT FOR PEACE.

IS OPENLY BISEXUAL AND A NATIONAL ROLE MODEL FOR THE UK'S LGBT COMMUNITY.

NO!

BRITISH BOXING BOARD OF CONTROL WOULD NOT GIVE OUT FIGHTING LICENSES TO WOMEN UNTIL 1998 BECAUSE THEY WRONGLY THOUGHT PMS WOULD MAKE WOMEN TOO EMOTIONALLY UNSTABLE.

HAS BEEN RANKED #1 IN ODI BATTING.

CAPTAIN OF INDIA'S WOMEN'S CRICKET TEAM.

MADE 214 RUNS IN 2002, BREAKING THE RECORD.

'I ALWAYS LOVE TO INTERACT WITH THE YOUTH AND IF I CAN MOTIVATE EVEN SOME OF THEM, I WILL FEEL BLESSED.' — MITHALI RAJ

# MITHALI RAJ

## CRICKET PLAYER

Mithali Raj was born in 1982 in Rajasthan, India. Growing up, she loved classical dance, but her father thought the discipline of cricket would be good for her. At first she missed dancing, but her talent was undeniable, and she would grow to love cricket and become a leader in the sport. Cricket is played on a large oval field with two wickets on opposite sides. Bowlers throw the ball to try to knock the wickets down, while a batter tries to hit the ball as hard as she can. Once the ball is hit, two batters make runs by switching sides as fast as they can before the opposite team knocks over their wickets. Mithali is a strong batter who also skilfully makes fast runs.

At age 14, Mithali was first standby for the World Cup. In 1999, she played in her first One-Day International game against Ireland, scoring 114 runs. At 19, she scored a record-breaking 214 runs during a test game against England. She was the best female batter in India and was appointed team captain.

In India, traditional gender roles still limit many women's options. Most of Mithali's teammates grew up without access to proper equipment. Mihali knew they needed wins to increase their funding. In 2005, she led her team to the World Cup finals, where they were beaten by Australia. In 2006, India won their first test series victory and won the Asia Cup.

In 2012, Mithali was ranked the world number one cricketer for one-day batting. Then came a series of losses for India, including a shattering defeat at the 2013 World Cup. But Mithali worked hard to bring the Indian women's team up in the rankings and gain respect in the public eye. For her hard work, she became the first woman to win the *Wisden India* Cricketer of the Year in 2015. That same year, she was also awarded one of India's highest civilian honours, the Padma Shri Award.

Mithali continues to be the face of women's cricket in India. She fights for gender equality and to create more opportunities for women in sport.

SECOND BATTER TO SCORE 5,000 RUNS IN WOMEN'S ONE-DAY INTERNATIONALS.

AT FIRST, HER EXTENDED FAMILY DIDN'T SUPPORT HER PLAYING CRICKET BECAUSE IT WAS 'UNLADYLIKE'.

FIGHTS FOR INDIAN WOMEN'S CRICKET TO GET MORE TV COVERAGE.

PLAYED FOR HYDERABAD IN DOMESTIC GAMES EARLY IN HER CAREER.

GIVEN THE ARJUNA AWARD BY THE INDIAN GOVERNMENT IN 2003.

ENCOURAGES GIRLS TO GET EDUCATED AND BE FINANCIALLY INDEPENDENT OF MEN.

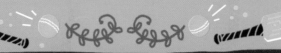

HAS MORE THAN 70 CAREER WINS.

WON HALFPIPE GOLD AT THE 2002 OLYMPICS AND BRONZE IN THE 2010 AND 2014 OLYMPICS.

WON 7 GOLD MEDALS AT THE X GAMES.

'I'VE NEVER BEEN VERY GOOD AT HOLDING BACK. I'VE NEVER BEEN VERY GOOD AT PLAYING IT SAFE... THERE'VE BEEN PEOPLE BETTER THAN ME MY ENTIRE LIFE. I JUST APPLIED MYSELF.' – KELLY CLARK

# KELLY CLARK

## SNOWBOARDER

Kelly Clark was born in 1983 and grew up playing in the snowy mountains of Vermont, USA. She started skiing at the age of two and was snowboarding by seven. Her talent led her to the Mount Snow Academy, where she could train while attending high school. Kelly would become the winningest snowboarder — male or female — in the history of the sport.

For half-pipe snowboarding, speed is key — the faster you go, the higher you can fly and the more impressive tricks you can do. Kelly needed plenty of amplitude (height) to stand out in this male-dominated sport. She grew fearless, daring to jump higher and make her tricks even bigger than her male competitors'. It paid off: in 2001 she won her first Grand Prix title.

In 2002, Kelly rocked the world of snowboarding, winning gold medals at the X Games and the Olympics, and winning the overall Grand Prix title. Her childhood dream of becoming an Olympic champion was fulfilled. The media couldn't get enough of their new champion.

At the next Olympics in 2006, Kelly was expected to defend her title. But travelling for publicity cut into her training time. Although she won gold at the 2006 X Games, she was not prepared enough for the Olympics and came in fourth. It was devastating, but she was resilient — she would train harder than ever to make it back on to the Olympic podium.

At the 2010 Olympics, she fell on her first run in the finals, but she didn't let that get her down. With more runs left, she amazed the judges with her tricks and landings — and won the bronze medal. She was prouder of this than of her Olympic gold because of all of the hard work that went into achieving it.

In 2013, she won her 60th career win, setting a new record in snowboarding. From 2002 to 2016, she won seven gold medals at the X Games and eight US Open titles, to name just a few of her triumphs. The world can't wait to see what she does next!

IN 2011, BECAME THE FIRST WOMAN TO LAND A 1080° DURING COMPETITION.

WON ESPY AWARDS IN 2002 AND 2015.

CREATED THE KELLY CLARK FOUNDATION, WHICH GIVES SCHOLARSHIPS TO YOUNG SNOWBOARDERS.

VIDEOTAPED THE FIRST OLYMPIC SNOWBOARDING EVENT SO SHE COULD WATCH IT AFTER SCHOOL.

HER HOMETOWN IN VERMONT PAINTED THEIR SNOWPLOUGH GOLD WHEN SHE WON HER OLYMPIC GOLD.

HAS WON 5 WORLD SNOWBOARD TOUR TITLES AND 6 US GRAND PRIX TITLES.

WON A GOLD AND A BRONZE MEDAL IN THE 2010 OLYMPICS.

FIRST SKIER EVER TO WIN 20 WORLD CUP CRYSTAL GLOBES.

HAS A RECORD-BREAKING 76 WORLD CUP WINS TO DATE.

'IF YOU'RE NOT FALLING, THEN YOU'RE DOING SOMETHING WRONG.' - LINDSEY VONN

# LINDSEY VONN

## ◀ ALPINE SKIER ▶

**HAS BEEN THE WORLD CUP DOWNHILL CHAMPION 8 TIMES.**

**INJURED HER KNEE AND COULDN'T COMPETE IN THE 2014 OLYMPICS, SO SHE COVERED IT ON THE NEWS INSTEAD**

**HAS WON 6 WORLD CHAMPIONSHIP MEDALS.**

Lindsey Caroline Vonn (née Kildow) was born in 1984 in Minnesota, USA and began skiing as a toddler. She started competing in international competitions at the age of nine.

At 17, Lindsey competed at the 2002 Olympics, placing sixth at the combined event. The following season, she won titles at the 2003 and 2004 US Championships. Back at the Olympics in 2006, Lindsey fell during a training run and had to be airlifted off the mountain. Luckily, no bones were broken, but she was in intense pain when she competed in her Olympic race two days later. She placed eighth, proud just to be able to compete.

In 2008, aged 20, she became the overall champion and downhill champion at the Alpine Skiing World Cup. She defended both titles the next year and won the Super-G event. In 2009, she won downhill and Super-G gold medals at the World Championships. She seemed unstoppable for the 2010 Olympics.

But one week before her arrival, she had another devastating crash landing and broke a shin bone. Luckily, bad weather delayed her race and allowed her more healing time. As she sped down the mountain during her event, she felt no pain, no nervousness, just pure focus on doing her very best. She came first, with a time of 1 minute, 44.19 seconds in the downhill race. As she crossed the finish line, she collapsed and raised her arms up to celebrate finally achieving her dream. She also won bronze in the Super-G event. By the end of 2010, she had also won her third Crystal Globe title, given to the racer with the most total points at the FIS Alpine Ski World Cup.

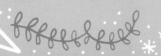

Lindsey Vonn continues to dominate the alpine skiing world, and is considered the world's greatest. In 2015, she set a new record with 67 World Cup wins, and to date she has 76 wins. She has proven that she is as tough as nails and, despite an injury, she will always get back up!

**WON THE ESPY AWARD FOR BEST FEMALE ATHLETE IN 2010 AND 2011.**

**THE LINDSEY VONN FOUNDATION HELPS TO EMPOWER GIRLS IN SPORT.**

**GOLFS FOR CHARITY.**

'I'M SCARED OF FAILURE ALL THE TIME, BUT NOT ENOUGH TO STOP TRYING.' — RONDA ROUSEY

# RONDA ROUSEY

## MIXED MARTIAL ARTS FIGHTER

Ronda Jean Rousey was born in 1987 and grew up in California, USA. Her mum was the first American World Judoka champion, and Ronda became a champion herself, winning gold at the 2007 Pan American Games and bronze at the 2008 Olympics.

After the intensity of Olympic training, she took a break from her judo career. She was unfocused, working multiple jobs, even living in her car at one point. But she returned to what she loved: fighting. This time it was Mixed Martial Arts (MMA). She started training at the Glendale Fighting Club. At first the club owner, Edmond Tarverdyan, didn't want to train her, but after months of observing her undeniable skill, Edmond decided to coach her for her 2010 MMA debut. He would continue to coach her throughout her career.

**FIRST AMERICAN WOMAN TO WIN AN OLYMPIC MEDAL IN JUDO.**

**ARM-BARRING IS HER SIGNATURE MOVE.**

At the time, there was not a large platform for women in professional MMA. People felt uncomfortable with women fighting so aggressively, breaking bones, and punching each other in the face. Many MMA fans thought the only women near the cage should be bikini-clad ring girls. Women fought in Strikeforce, a professional organisation smaller than the Ultimate Fighting Championship. Pioneers like Gina Carano and Julie Kedzie proved their worth in some of the first televised female MMA fights, paving the way for Ronda.

**HER MEMOIR IS CALLED MY FIGHT/YOUR FIGHT.**

In 2011, Ronda was undefeated in amateur MMA and ready to go pro in Strikeforce. After winning four pro fights, Ronda challenged the champion, Miesha Tate, and in 2012, Ronda defeated Miesha to become the new Strikeforce champion. Later that year, mainly because of Ronda's performance in Strikeforce, the UFC started its first women's division. Ronda was named the first female UFC Bantamweight Champion and became a star of MMA. Her pro fights usually end in less than a minute; the fastest was 14 seconds, the shortest match in UFC history.

**NICKNAMED 'ROWDY'.**

**PLAYED AN ACTION STAR IN THE MOVIES FURIOUS 7 AND THE EXPENDABLES 3.**

Ronda defended her UFC title for three years. She is a role model as one of the best in a male-dominated sport.

4-TIME WOMEN'S MOTOCROSS CHAMPION.

FIRST DEAF PROFESSIONAL MOTOCROSS RIDER.

WON 2 GOLD MEDALS AT THE X GAMES.

FIRST AMERICAN WOMAN TO EARN A FACTORY RIDE.

'I DON'T LOOK AT MYSELF AS DIFFERENT. I JUST CAN'T HEAR, AND THAT'S WHO I AM. I JUST LOVE TO RACE.' — ASHLEY FIOLEK

# ASHLEY FIOLEK

## MOTOCROSS RIDER

Ashley Fiolek was born in 1990 in Michigan, USA. When she was diagnosed with profound deafness, her parents learned sign language and got involved in the Deaf community. They saw Ashley's deafness not as something wrong with her, but as something that made her unique.

Ashley's father and grandfather were both motocross riders, and at the age of seven, she rode in her first motocross bike race. She was a natural.

WOW!

Motocross riders usually depend on hearing their engine to tell when to switch gears. Most listen to tell if a driver is gaining on them or about to cut them off. Ashley learned to depend on her other senses — to scan the track for shadows to spot her competition and to switch gears based on her motor's vibration instead of its sound. At first, parents of other riders were afraid that a Deaf rider could put their kids in danger, but once they saw Ashley's winning performances, they changed their minds. At 17, she went pro. She won gold medals at the 2009 and 2010 X Games, and by 2011, she had won titles at three Women's Motocross Association (WMA) championships.

Ashley's ultimate goal was to compete in men's motocross racing. But before she got the opportunity, things started to change in the WMA. In 2011, motocross began airing on live TV, but only the men's pro races. Without TV exposure, women's racing was largely unknown to the general public. Women's races were often scheduled for the end of the day, when the crowds start leaving. Sponsors weren't interested, so organisers started getting rid of women's pro racing. This meant no more pro sponsorships. Ashley had had enough. Feeling women were not getting a fair shot, she left motocross racing after winning the 2012 WMA championship. Ashley continues to ride as a stuntwoman and tours the USA telling her story. She still loves her bike and would race again, but only in a situation offering female racers the same opportunity given to men in the sport.

ASHLEY FEELS 'ONE WITH THE BIKE' AND SHIFTING GEARS BASED ON ENGINE VIBRATIONS HAS BECOME INSTINCTIVE.

WON A WMA CHAMPIONSHIP WITH A BROKEN COLLARBONE.

HER DAD WAS HER COACH.

WAS IN THE MARVEL UNIVERSE LIVE TOUR.

WITHOUT THE NOISE OF THE CROWD OR THE BIKES, SHE FEELS PEACEFUL AND ZEN-LIKE ON THE TRACK.

WON GOLD IN THE 2012 AND 2016 OLYMPICS.

BMX WORLD CHAMPION.

FIRST PERSON FROM COLOMBIA TO WIN A GOLD MEDAL IN THE OLYMPICS FOR BMX.

'THE EMOTION YOU FEEL IS JUST IMPOSSIBLE TO EXPLAIN ... SEEING MY FLAG GO UP AND HEARING MY NATIONAL ANTHEM IN ANOTHER COUNTRY MADE ME FEEL MORE COLOMBIAN THAN EVER.' —MARIANA PAJÓN ON WINNING HER FIRST OLYMPIC GOLD MEDAL

# MARIANA PAJÓN

## ⚙ BMX CYCLIST ⚙

Mariana Pajón Londoño was born in 1991 and grew up in Medellín, Colombia. Mariana's dad and brother were both bicycle motocross (BMX) racers; she started riding aged four and racing aged nine. Usually she was the only girl in the race and would beat all the boys. Before long, she would become world champion.

BMX is an extreme, high-speed sport. Riders are released from a steep slope and race around a dirt track with many obstacles and jumps. Riders spend the whole race standing up on the bike to get the most force from their legs. BMX is also a contact sport: pile-ups and broken bones are not uncommon.

To become a BMX champion, Mariana trained up to eight hours a day to build power in her legs, much like a sprinter would. In 2008, aged 16, she won her first world title. She went on to win the Junior World Championship title again the next year, and the World Championship in 2010 and 2011. She won gold medals at the 2010 Central American and the South American Games and the 2011 Pan American Games in Mexico. Mariana was the top-ranking BMX biker in the world, and at age 20 qualified for the 2012 Olympics, her lifelong goal.

In a BMX race, eight competing riders must stick to their lane for the first and last parts of the race. In her final Olympic race, Mariana raced in the fourth lane, not her favourite. But she decided just to ride her best and enjoy being at the Olympics. When the gates were released, she soon worked her way into the lead, and she just had to execute all of her jumps perfectly to win. No one could catch up with her, and she won the gold! Mariana was filled with pride for her country and the joy of fulfilling a dream.

After her 2012 victory, Mariana continued to dominate the BMX world, winning gold medals at several World Championships and the 2016 Olympics. She is truly the queen of BMX!

**CARRIED THE COLOMBIAN FLAG DURING THE 2012 OLYMPIC PARADE.**

**AS A KID, SHE WANTED TO BE AN OLYMPIC GYMNAST.**

**IN 2011, COLOMBIA NAMED HER SPORTSWOMAN OF THE YEAR.**

**NICKNAMED THE QUEEN OF BMX, THE BMX BANDIT AND THE DIRT QUEEN.**

**EL COMPLEJO MARIANA PAJÓN**

**A BMX RIDING COMPLEX IS NAMED AFTER HER.**

**SECOND PERSON FROM COLOMBIA TO WIN AN OLYMPIC GOLD MEDAL.**

HAS SET OVER 13 WORLD RECORDS.

HAS WON 9 WORLD CHAMPIONSHIP GOLD MEDALS.

HAS WON 5 OLYMPIC GOLD MEDALS AND 1 SILVER MEDAL IN HER CAREER SO FAR.

'THE SWIMMER MINDSET IS ALWAYS TO IMPROVE ON YOUR BEST, YOUR PERSONAL

# KATIE LEDECKY

## SWIMMER

Kathleen Genevieve 'Katie' Ledecky was born in 1997 in Washington, DC, USA. Her mum taught her how to swim as a toddler, and she joined her first swimming team aged six. That's when she started setting goals in a journal where she recorded her 'want times'. She enjoyed noting her improving swim times and meeting each new challenge. As Katie grew up, she became known for her strong work ethic, cheerful personality and speed in the pool.

Her hard work paid off: aged just 15 she qualified for the Olympic trials and earned a spot on the US team at the 2012 Games. Her new goal was Olympic gold. At the Games, Katie won her first gold, in the 800 m race, breaking the previously held American record. She was a sensation!

Katie would become unstoppable. In 2013, she won four gold medals at the World Championships, and in 2014, she won gold medals in all five of her events at the Pan Pacific Championships, including the 800 m relay, the 200 m, the 400 m, the 800 m, and, most impressive and intense of all, the 1500 m. At the 2015 World Championships, she also won five gold medals in these events. No other athlete has swept golds like this at either of those competitions. All the while, she set new world records, even breaking her own previous records.

At the 2016 Olympics, she shocked the world by medalling in every event she competed in. She set new world record times and won gold in the 200 m, 400 m and 800 m freestyle events. She also won gold in the 4x200 m relay and silver in the 4x100 m relay.

WORLD RECORD!

In her short career, Katie Ledecky has already become a legend. Rarely out of the water for long, she can be found practising and working on her next goal, beating her own records and chasing her own personal best.

ONE OF KATIE'S TECHNIQUES IS CALLED A 'LOPING' OR 'GIDDY UP' STROKE.

—TIME—

WAS THE YOUNGEST PERSON ON THE 2016 TIME 100 LIST.

WON THE FEMALE ATHLETE OF THE YEAR GOLDEN GOGGLE AWARD FROM 2013–2015.

DESCRIBES HERSELF AS 'A DISTANCE SWIMMER WITH A SPRINTER'S MENTALITY'.

HER MUM SWAM FOR THE UNIVERSITY OF NEW MEXICO.

HAS EARNED OVER 20 MEDALS IN MAJOR INTERNATIONAL COMPETITIONS.

'I'M NOT THE NEXT USAIN BOLT OR MICHAEL PHELPS. I'M THE FIRST SIMONE BILES.' — SIMONE BILES

# SIMONE BILES

## GYMNAST

Simone Biles runs at full speed to catapult herself into the air. First she does a round-off, straight into a back handspring and then she is flying and flipping twice with legs straight. She moves seamlessly in the air, and at the very last minute does a half twist and sticks a blind landing. This manoeuvre, called 'the Biles', is the signature move of one of the greatest gymnasts in the history of the sport. It requires so much power that most male gymnasts can't even do it.

Simone Arianne Biles was born in 1997 in Ohio, USA. As a toddler, she went to live with her grandparents, who soon adopted Simone and her sister, becoming their mum and dad. Simone was always jumping around the house, doing flips and tricks. She tried gymnastics for the first time aged six on a field trip to a gym. The coaches immediately noticed her natural talent, and she began training.

In 2013, she won the World Gymnastics Championship for the first time. She defended her title in 2014 and 2015, making her the first woman to win all-around gymnastic titles at the World Championships three years in a row. She then earned a spot on the 2016 US team for the Olympic Games in Rio de Janeiro. The pressure was on, and she would not disappoint.

Her 2016 Olympic floor routine included 'the Biles' as well as other tricky manoeuvres like a double layout with a full twist or a double-tucked flip with two twists. By the end, Simone often couldn't feel her legs but still had a huge smile.

In Rio, Simone performed with perfection and became a household name. She won gold in the vault, floor exercise, individual all-around and team all-around. She also won bronze on the balance beam. Simone is having the time of her life, twisting and flipping as she soars through the air, and her millions of fans can't wait to see what she does next!

HAS WON 4 ALL-AROUND NATIONAL TITLES.

'THE BILES' IS NAMED AFTER HER BECAUSE SHE IS THE FIRST PERSON TO LAND THE MANOEUVRE IN COMPETITION.

HOLDS A WORLD-RECORD 10 WORLD CHAMPIONSHIP GOLD MEDALS.

SHE STANDS 4'8 TALL.

EATS PIZZA AFTER EVERY MEET!

HER COACH, AIMEE BOORMAN, HAS BEEN TRAINING HER SINCE SHE WAS 8 AND IS LIKE SIMONE'S 2ND MUM.

# MORE WOMEN IN SPORT

## DONNA LOPIANO
### 1946 -

Six-time national champion, nine-time All-American and three-time MVP softball player. She was the CEO of the Women's Sports Foundation.

## DIANA NYAD
### 1949 -

This fearless athlete became the first person to swim from Cuba to Florida without a shark cage — at age 64!

## NANCY LOPEZ
### 1957 -

One of the greatest female golfers in history, she's won 48 LPGA events and countless awards and entered the World Golf Hall of Fame in 1987.

## LAILA ALI
### 1977 -

The daughter of boxing legend Muhammad Ali, she is undefeated, having boxed 24 fights and won all of them, 21 of them by knockouts.

## KERRI STRUG
### 1977 -

She inspired the world when she vaulted with a badly sprained ankle at the 1996 Olympics. She landed on one foot and took home the gold medal.

## MISTY MAY-TREANOR
### 1977 -
## KERRI WALSH JENNINGS
### 1978 -

Considered the best-ever two-playe beach volleyball team, they won 112 games and three Olympic gold medal

## ANNIE SMITH PECK
### 1850 -1935

In a time when women were not expected to be active, Annie climbed some of the world's very tallest mountains.

## ORA WASHINGTON
### 1898 -1971

Called the 'Queen of Tennis', she won the American Tennis Association singles eight times and the doubles 12 times.

## MARGARET MURDOCK
### 1942 -

In the 1967 Pan American Games, she broke the men's record in small-bore shooting. She also won a silver medal at the 1976 Olympics.

## FLORENCE GRIFFITH-JOYNER
### 1959 -

She won three gold medals and one silver medal at the 1988 Olympics. She set the still-standing records for the 100 m and 200 m races.

## CAMILLE DUVALL
### 1960 -

The waterskier has won the Pro Tournament championship 43 times. Named one of the '100 Greatest Female Athletes of the Century'.

## KRISTIN ARMSTRONG
### 1973 -

She was a triathlete but developed osteoarthritis. She turned to cycling and won gold at the 2008, 2012 and 2016 Olympics, plus two World Championships.

## FU MINGXIA
### 1978 -

A few days from her 14th birthday, she won her first Olympic gold medal in 1992. She won two more in 1996 and a gold in diving and a silver in synchronised diving in 2000.

## MICHELLE KWAN
### 1980 -

One of the winningest women in American figure-skating with five world titles, nine national titles and two Olympic medals.

## PAMELA ROSA
### 1999 -

In 2016, this Brazilian 16-year-old became the youngest champion of the X Games in the Skateboard Street event. She won silver at the 2014 and 2015 X Games.

# CONCLUSION

Throughout history, women have had to jump further, run faster and fight harder to prove their worth in the sporting arena. Women make up half of the world's population, and each individual has unique skills and strengths that should be celebrated. But women and girls have traditionally been told that they are weak and that beauty is the only aspect of their physical self they should be concerned about. The athletes in this book busted through these stereotypes to show that women are not fragile and their bodies are not weak; they are fierce competitors.

These women faced huge challenges but with each world record and feat of strength, they showed the world what women are capable of. They proved that there is nothing more 'ladylike' than training the hardest, sweating the most and striving for greatness. They became role models for women and girls around the world, inspiring girls to pursue their passions.

So ask yourself: What is my next victory? Play hard, keep up that hustle and don't be afraid to dream big, because you are strong.

# ACKNOWLEDGEMENTS

First, I want to thank all of the brave women who pursued their passions in sport. They have pushed — and continue to push — themselves to their limits to become the very best athletes they can be. Because of their hard work, we can debunk the myth that women's bodies are weak.

A huge thank you to all the girls out there who are giving it their all on the field, in the pool, on the court and beyond. I am so excited to see what new records you will break and how you will shock and change the world with your achievements.

I want to thank my amazing team at Ten Speed Press, including the best editor in all space and time, Kaitlin Ketchum; the wonderful and talented publicist Daniel Wikey; and the typesetting wizards and designers Tatiana Pavlova and Lizzie Allen. Thank you so much for your talent and hard work, making this book possible! And a big thank you to my awesome agent, Monica Odom, for all of her support!

I also want to thank my parents and my baseball-playing brother Adam Ignotofsky, who put up with a lifetime of having an 'indoor kid' older sister. A big thank you to Aditya Voleti for his great suggestions and help with fact-checking, and for all our midnight walks. A thank you to Lauren Hale for her great suggestions during many happy hours. And a huge I love you and thank you to my husband, Thomas Mason IV, for supporting and feeding me during all of my late-night drawing sessions and for teaching me once and for all how to ride a bike.

# ABOUT THE AUTHOR

Rachel Ignotofsky is a *New York Times* bestselling author and illustrator who is proud to share the stories of amazing women with the world. Her first book, *Women in Science*, has encouraged both kids and adults to learn more about the groundbreaking female scientists who changed our world. With *Women in Sport*, Rachel wants everyone to learn how these fierce athletes fought to pursue their passions and change perceptions about what women's bodies are capable of.

Rachel grew up in New Jersey, USA on a healthy diet of cartoons and pudding, and graduated with honours from Tyler School of Art's graphic design programme in 2011. Now based in Kansas City, Missouri, Rachel works for herself and spends all day and night drawing, writing and learning as much as she can. Her work is inspired by history and science. She believes that illustration is a powerful tool that can make learning exciting, and she has a passion for taking dense information and making it fun and accessible.

To learn more about Rachel, visit her website at: www.rachelignotofskydesign.com.

# SOURCES

Researching this book was so much fun. I used all sorts of sources: newspapers, interviews, lectures, books, films and the internet! News articles and obituaries were key to learning about the stories of these amazing women. If you're interested in learning more about these women (and you definitely should!), here are some of the sources I consulted, which are great places to start.

## BOOKS

Bryant, Jill. *Women Athletes Who Changed the World (Great Women of Achievement)*. New York: Rosen Pub., 2012.

Dixon, Joan. *Trailblazing Sports Heroes: Exceptional Personalities and Outstanding Achievements in Canadian Sport*. Canmore, AL: Altitude Pub. Canada, 2003.

Garg, Chitra. *Indian Champions: Profiles of Famous Indian Sportspersons*. Kashmere Gate, Delhi: Rajpal & Sons, 2010.

Hasday, Judy L. *Extraordinary Women Athletes (Extraordinary People)*. New York: Children's Press, 2000.

McDougall, Chros. *Girls Play to Win Figure Skating*. Chicago: Norwood House Press, 2011.

Rappoport, Ken. *Ladies First: Women Athletes Who Made a Difference*. Atlanta: Peachtree, 2005.

Woolum, Janet. *Outstanding Women Athletes: Who They Are and How They Influenced Sports in America*. Phoenix, AZ: Oryx Press, 1992.

## STATISTICS

Cooky, Cheryl, Michael A. Messner, and Michela Musto. "It's Dude Time!: A Quarter Century of Excluding Women's Sports in Televised News and Highlight Shows." *Communication & Sport* 2167479515588761, first published on June 5, 2015 doi:10.1177/2167479515588761.

Good, Andrew. "When It Comes to Women in Sports, TV News Tunes Out." *USC News*. June 5, 2015. https://news.usc.edu/82382/when-it-comes-to-women-in-sports-tv-news-tunes-out/. Accessed October 17, 2016.

Isidore, Chris. "Women World Cup Champs Win Waaay Less Money than Men." *CNNMoney*. July 7, 2015. http://money.cnn.com/2015/07/07/news/companies/womens-world-cup-prize-money/. Accessed October 17, 2016

Pilon, Mary. "The World Cup Pay Gap, What the U.S. and Japan Didn't Win in the Women's Soccer Final." *POLITICO Comments*. July 06, 2015. http://www.politico.eu/article/world-cup-women-pay-gap-gender-equality/. Accessed October 17, 2016.

Walters, John. "Taking a Closer Look at the Gender Gap in Sports." *Newsweek*. January 4, 2016. http://www.newsweek.com/womens-soccer-suit-underscores-sports-gender-pay-gap-443137. Accessed October 17, 2016.

Womens Sports Foundation. "Pay Inequity in Athletics." July 20, 2015. https://www.womenssportsfoundation.org/research/article-and-report/equity-issues/pay-inequity/. Accessed October 17, 2016.

# WEBSITES

*Encyclopedia Britannica*: www.britannica.com

ESPN Cricket Info: www.espncricinfo.com

ESPN SportsCentury: www.espn.go.com/sportscentury

*Guardian* obituaries: www.theguardian.com/tone/obituaries

*Los Angeles Times* obituaries: obituaries.latimes.com

Olympic.org: www.olympic.org

Makers, the largest video collection of women's stories: www.makers.com

National Museum of Racing and Hall of Fame: www.racingmuseum.org

*New York Times* obituaries: www.nytimes.com/section/obituaries

Rio 2016 NBC Olympics: www.nbcolympics.com

*Sports Illustrated* Vault: www.si.com/vault

Team USA: www.teamusa.org

TED Women: www.ted.com/topics/women

USA Gymnastics: https://usagym.org

U.S. Soccer: www.ussoccer.com

VICE Sports: https://sports.vice.com/en_us

Women's Sports Foundation: www.womenssportsfoundation.org

World Archery: https://worldarchery.org

X Games: xgames.espn.com

# SOURCES

Here are some of the more specific articles and videos that I thought were super-interesting and helped me write this book.

Bernstein, Viv. "Susan Butcher, Pioneer in Sled-Dog Racing, Is Dead at 51." *New York Times*. April 7, 2006. http://www.nytimes.com/2006/08/07/sports/07butcher.html. Accessed October 16, 2016.

"Best Olympic Archers of All-Time: #1 Kim Soo-Nyung." World Archery. July 07, 2016. https://worldarchery.org/news/142020/best-olympic-archers-all-time-1-kim-soo-nyung. Accessed October 17, 2016.

"Bev Francis." IFBB Professional League. http://www.ifbbpro.com/bev-francis/. Accessed October 16, 2016.

"Billie Jean King: This Tennis Icon Paved the Way for Women in Sports." Ted Women. May 2015. https://www.ted.com/talks/billie_jean_king_this_tennis_icon_paved_the_way_for_women_in_sports?language=en. Accessed October 16, 2016.

Costantinou, Marianne. "Ann Calvello, The Flamboyant Villainess of Roller Derby." SFGate. March 16, 2006. http://www.sfgate.com/bayarea/article/Ann-Calvello-the-flamboyant-villainess-of-2501749.php. Accessed October 16, 2016.

Day, Peter. "Why Ellen MacArthur Is Still Going round in Circles." BBC News. January 23, 2015. http://www.bbc.com/news/business-30912769. Accessed October 17, 2016.

Dumas, Daisy. "Winning Approach: Surf Champion Layne Beachley on What Drives Her." *Sydney Morning Herald*. March 11, 2016. http://www.smh.com.au/nsw/brunch-with-layne-beachley-20160309-gnep85.html. Accessed October 17, 2016.

Fincher, Julia. "Who is... Simone Biles." NBC Olympics. July 29, 2016. http://www.nbcolympics.com/news/who-simone-biles. Accessed January 17, 2017.

Hanser, Kathleen. "Georgia "Tiny" Broadwick's Parachute." National Air and Space Museum. March 12, 2015. https://airandspace.si.edu/stories/editorial/georgia-"tiny"-broadwick's-parachute. Accessed October 16, 2016.

Hedegaard, Erik. "Ronda Rousey: The World's Most Dangerous Woman." *Rolling Stone*. May 28, 2015. http://www.rollingstone.com/sports/features/ronda-rousey-the-worlds-most-dangerous-woman-20150528. Accessed January 17, 2017.

Horn, Robert. "No Mountain Too High For Her, Junko Tabei Defied Japanese Views Of Women To Become An Expert Climber." *Sports Illustrated*. April 29, 1996. http://www.si.com/vault/1996/04/29/212374/no-mountain-too-high-for-her-junko-tabei-defied-japanese-views-of-women-to-become-an-expert-climber. Accessed October 16, 2016.

Howard, Johnette. "The Right Woman for the Job." ESPNW. December 1, 2013. http://www.espn.com/espnw/news-commentary/article/10044322/espnw-nba-ref-violet-palmer-paved-way-other-women. Accessed October 16, 2016.

Hussain, Leila, and Matthew Knight. "Valentina Vezzali: Olympic Fencer Turned Political Jouster." CNN. April 22, 2015. http://edition.cnn.com/2015/04/22/sport/valentina-vezzali-fencing-olympics-italy/. Accessed October 17, 2016.

Khaleeli, Homa. "Nicola Adams: 'It always felt like boxing was my path'" *Guardian Saturday interview*. August 08, 2014. https://www.theguardian.com/sport/2014/aug/08/nicola-adams-boxing-was-my-path. Accessed January 17, 2017.

Kloke, Joshua. "Manon Rheaume Remains an Inspiration to Female Hockey Players." VICE Sports. June 20, 2015. https://sports.vice.com/en_us/article/manon-rheaume-remains-an-inspiration-to-female-hockey-players. Accessed October 17, 2016.

Litsky, Frank. "Aileen Riggin Soule, Olympic Diver and Swimmer, Dies at 96." *New York Times*. October 21, 2002. http://www.nytimes.com/2002/10/21/sports/aileen-riggin-soule-olympic-diver-and-swimmer-dies-at-96.html. Accessed October 16, 2016.

"Pajón focused on retaining BMX crown." International Olympic Committee. June 23, 2016. https://www.olympic.org/news/pajon-focused-on-retaining-bmx-crown. Accessed January 17, 2017

Price, S.L. "Back to her roots: How Katie Ledecky became so dominant in the pool." *Sports Illustrated*. June 1, 2016. http://www.si.com/olympics/2016/06/01/olympics-2016-road-to-rio-katie-ledecky-swimming. Accessed January 17, 2017.

Roenigk, Alyssa. "Silence is Golden." ESPN. January 27, 2010. http://www.espn.com/action/news/story?id=4227966. Accessed January 17, 2017.

Siljeg, Sky. "A Talk with Patti McGee, "The First Betty" of Skateboarding on Going Pro." Scholastic. http://teacher.scholastic.com/scholasticnews/indepth/skateboarding/articles/index.asp?article=patti. Accessed October 16, 2016.

"Syers Skates to Landmark Gold." International Olympic Committee. https://www.olympic.org/news/syers-skates-to-landmark-gold. Accessed October 16, 2016.

Thomas, Robert MCG., Jr. "Toni Stone, 75, First Woman To Play Big-League Baseball ..." *New York Times*. November 10, 1996. http://www.nytimes.com/1996/11/10/sports/toni-stone-75-first-woman-to-play-big-league-baseball.html. Accessed October 16, 2016.

Thompson, Anna. "Women's Sport Pioneers: Cyclist Beryl Burton." BBC Sport. March 2, 2015. http://www.bbc.com/sport/cycling/31641006. Accessed October 16, 2016.

Trans World Sport. "Kelly Clark US Snowboarding Sensation." YouTube. January 20, 2015. https://www.youtube.com/watch?v=rt72QMByBg8. Accessed January 17, 2017.

Woo, Elaine. "Sue Sally Hale, 65; First Woman of Polo Played 20 Years in Disguise." *Los Angeles Times*. May 01, 2003. http://articles.latimes.com/2003/may/01/local/me-hale1. Accessed October 16, 2016.

Yardley, William. "Keiko Fukuda, a Trailblazer in Judo, Dies at 99." *New York Times*. February 16, 2013. http://www.nytimes.com/2013/02/17/sports/keiko-fukuda-99-a-trailblazer-in-judo-is-dead.html. Accessed October 16, 2016.

# INDEX

DEDICATED TO THOMAS.

PUBLISHED IN GREAT BRITAIN IN 2018 BY WREN & ROOK
FIRST PUBLISHED IN THE UNITED STATES IN 2017 BY TEN SPEED PRESS

COPYRIGHT © 2017 RACHEL IGNOTOFSKY
PUBLISHED BY ARRANGEMENT WITH TEN SPEED PRESS, AN IMPRINT OF
THE CROWN PUBLISHING GROUP, A DIVISION OF PENGUIN RANDOM HOUSE LLC

ISBN: 978 1 5263 6092 2
EBOOK ISBN: 978 1 5263 6093 9
10 9 8 7 6 5 4 3 2 1

WREN & ROOK
AN IMPRINT OF
HACHETTE CHILDREN'S GROUP
PART OF HODDER & STOUGHTON
CARMELITE HOUSE
50 VICTORIA EMBANKMENT
LONDON EC4Y 0DZ

AN HACHETTE UK COMPANY
WWW.HACHETTE.CO.UK
WWW.HACHETTECHILDRENS.CO.UK

PRINTED IN CHINA

THE WEBSITE ADDRESSES (URLS) INCLUDED IN THIS
BOOK WERE VALID AT THE TIME OF GOING TO PRESS.
HOWEVER, IT IS POSSIBLE THAT CONTENTS OR ADDRESSES
MAY HAVE CHANGED SINCE THE PUBLICATION OF THIS
BOOK. NO RESPONSIBILITY FOR ANY SUCH CHANGES CAN
BE ACCEPTED BY EITHER THE AUTHOR OR THE PUBLISHER.